OVER THE MOON BY CHRISTMAS

Sue Guy.

OVER THE MOON BY CHRISTMAS

PAMELA WELTON

Published by Pamela Welton

ISBN: 978-0-9562847-0-9

Book designed and produced for the publisher by Gleam Press, UK.
www.gleampress.com | info@gleampress.com

Printed in the United Kingdom

For communications concerning this book or to order copies please contact:
marmsspg@aol.com

Dedicated to Robert and my family

Contents

Foreword

If you are looking for glib, easy answers to life's riddles, you will not find them here! The story of Pamela and John does not fit neatly into the pre-arranged theological boxes of much contemporary Christianity. Rather, their experience is a journey of discovery, painfully negotiated, for which there are few maps. What does emerge from the pages is the triumph of trust and love over bewildering adversity, debilitating oppression and constant pain.

However, the reader will find also a story that celebrates the wonder and innocence of childhood, the joys and perils of family life and the blessing of treasured and faithful friendships along the way. It is told simply with humour, warmth and great charm. Both victories and setbacks litter the path and hope is frequently deferred, then re-awakened, as God leads a young family, new in the faith, through the trials and tribulations of following Jesus. It is a story that is recounted honestly, graciously and compassionately as human sin and frailty, loss and brokenness, disappointment and heartbreak, alongside physical distress, depression and paralysing fear are laid bare, yet touched by God's forgiveness, grace and healing.

Sometimes, Pamela and John witness and experience God's supernatural power intervening directly in their lives; at other times, more indirectly, bringing protection and provision in marvellous ways. What some might call "coin-cidence" faith sees as evidence of His caring hand. Yet, on other occasions, God inexplicably leaves them to struggle, seemingly alone and forgotten in the dark amid many doubts. How many of us can identify with such heights and depths, both assaults and assurances? Yet, through it all, we also have to learn to trust God, who is Lord of all circum-stances, and know He is with us constantly working out His perfect plan for our lives.

> *Therefore, my dear friends, as you have always obeyed — not only in my presence, but now much more in my absence — continue to work out your salvation with fear and trembling, for it is God who works in you to will and to act according to his good purpose. Philippians 2:12-13.*

Pamela and John know something of "fear and trem-bling" and I trust that these pages will bring needed encour-agement to many and a timely reassurance that God is at work in us for His good pleasure. We do have to "work out" our salvation and Pamela and John have had to make decisions and choices along the way, to turn from wrong paths and dead ends in order to embrace God's will for their lives; such is authentic Christian discipleship! There have been mentors on the journey but the sacrifices have had to be their own. The fruit, thus far, can be seen in their lives, in the lives of their children now grown up, and in the many others whose lives they have intersected with and affected for good on the path.

Pamela's story does not promise that all will be sorted out in this life, the battle still goes on, but it does point us to Jesus as the One who is always faithful, always loving and always with us. You may or may not know Him yet, just as Pamela and John did not when this pilgrimage of theirs began, but He is present whether we know Him or not, and watching over all of us. However, His desire is that we should come to know and love Him, in a growing manner, as He already knows and loves us intimately, completely, and unreservedly.

My hope and prayer, together with Pamela's and John's own, is that these pages will help all who read them to know that there is a God, and to learn to journey with Him alongside them in their own story.

Paul Miller,
April 2007

Chapter 1

The Journey Begins

I stood in my dressing gown and kissed them "goodbye" and watched as the two little figures held hands and became gradually smaller as they walked away down the long, stark corridor. Wrapped up for winter in their furry, grey duffle coats, they looked like Paddington bears, needing each other as they had never done before. At the end of the corridor, a tall figure stood waiting to take them away and I waved as they turned around and waved "goodbye." This was my family, my husband John, Charlie aged five and Sam aged three, separated from me by a sudden nightmare.

I was left feeling so alone, looking at the melted After-Eight mint in my hand, a little offering of love and comfort that they had brought. There was so much whirling through my mind. Worries that any mother would have. What about their washing? What about their dinner money? Would John be able to look after them? Even worse were the greater concerns that were non-existent at the start of the day. Would I live to see them grow up?

I returned to my room in the Neurosurgical hospital to take in what had happened. I could see the car park through a large window and my small case on a chair, containing essentials that I had asked John to bring .... my teddy, nightclothes, wash bag and a colourful well-read Bible that I had never looked at. It seemed at a time of trauma such as this that it might be of help. Some people must have found comfort in it but not me.

I reflected on the day. It was a day that I had expected to find difficult but hoped would provide a solution to my problem. For eight weeks, I had been in excruciating pain in my face, eyes, and ears, and I could take no more. My father was a doctor and so it was natural for me to turn to him for advice when the usual painkillers had no effect. After eight weeks I was feeling suicidal with pain and so he referred me to a consultant he respected. I had a morning outpatient appointment at his pain clinic and so it was easy to take Charlie and Sam to nursery and then go to the hospital. I was full of hope for a way out of pain and I wanted to be well in order to prepare for Christmas so that the boys could enjoy the celebrations that I had always loved so much as a child.

Travelling on the bus, I felt nervous. I had heard that the consultant had a reputation of being severe and I had never liked hospitals but it would be worth it to end this pain. I felt uncomfortable as I passed the old-fashioned, concrete wards and a strange feeling of imprisonment covered me. I looked forward to catching the bus home, carrying a miracle drug that would remove my pain. After all, whenever I was ill as a child my father gave me a tablet and I got better. Doctors could solve any problem. Nothing had prepared me for what was to come.

"The Prof," as the consultant was known, sat behind his desk wearing a stiff white coat and a serious expression that added to his air of authority. It was obvious that here was a man who was used to being obeyed. On either side of him sat a junior doctor. I called them "nodding dog doctors" because whatever he said they nodded in agreement but said nothing. They were like the toy dogs people placed on the back shelf of their cars, nodding because of the movement and yet inanimate. I sat down as "The Prof" read my referral letter and I was surprised that as he looked at me I could detect a look of compassion in his eyes. He asked me about my pain and the details of how it began and made notes. He then wanted to measure my pain and how severe it was. A nurse attached a blood pressure cuff to my upper arm and began to tighten it, asking me to tell her when the pain in my arm was greater than the pain in my head. I could not work out how I could assess this but eventually the pain of the tightening cuff became so great that I became unaware of the pain in my head. That, I assumed, was what they wanted to know.

The nodding dog doctors made respectful noises and gestures as "The Prof" commented on his observations, then my shock came.

"I'm sorry, my dear," he said with concern in his voice and a look of softness in his eyes despite the stern expression and air of authority. "Your pain is so severe that I cannot allow you to go home. Arrange for someone to bring in what you need and I will arrange a bed for you."

I was stunned. All I wanted was a tablet for the pain. The numbness quickly turned to panic as all the routine and arrangements for the boys raced through my head. I needed to go home. "I have to go home," I protested, "I have children to meet from nursery."

"I'm sorry my dear," was his firm reply, "It would be too dangerous for you. You have to stay."

I could not understand. "Why?" I pleaded.

"I fear that you may have a brain tumour or an aneurysm," he explained. "If it is an aneurysm there is a danger of a blood vessel in your brain bursting so you need to be here."

Still desperate to go home and panicking, I continued my questions. "If it bursts what would happen?" I persisted, thinking I would find a way around the situation. "The Prof" was honest and direct.

"You will die," he said firmly. Die! The thought had never entered my head. "When?" I asked feeling more shocked and bewildered.

"At any moment," was his reply mixed with concern but a cool distancing from the emotion of the moment.

I have always been a person who has to have a plan and likes to know the facts. I need to know details and cannot handle "maybes." So the consultation continued with my mouth and brain obviously working even though a million possibilities and potential problems milled around in my head.

"If it's a brain tumour what will happen?" I asked, gathering information to make a plan and stay in control.

"We may be able to operate but that will depend on where the tumour is located. If we cannot operate you will die," was his response. I needed and respected his honesty and directness. I needed facts.

"How long might I live?" I continued.

"I cannot say exactly but I would estimate about three months."

I realized I had no choice but to stay and even if I had a choice, the authority this man carried was such that no one would go against his advice. Suddenly, in one hour an ordinary but different day had changed my life for ever. At the age of thirty, I was facing death.

A kindly nurse guided me, numb, from the room. Everything seemed to move into slow motion as I tried to work out the priorities and what I needed to do. My first concern was for the boys but I realized I would have to notify John, my husband. I never phoned him at work feeling that his job was far too important to be interrupted by domestic problems, and although he loved the boys he never had much to do with their upbringing (maybe because I had not let him). He was also so busy. But now we needed him as never before. I could not handle this alone. I had change for the bus home in my bag and so I decided to use it in the public phone box to call him. I was too shocked to tell him the news gently so I just told him as it was, and we arranged for him to collect Charlie and Sam. I also asked him to bring in a case of necessities, my teddy who went everywhere to remind me of home and just in case, the colourful Bible. Facing death, I reckoned that if there was a God now was the time I would be needing Him and people seemed to find the Bible useful.

The rest of the day passed in a haze of confusion, fear, panic, and worry ending with me in bed, my hand covered in chocolate, my face covered in tears through which I surveyed the small room I had been placed in. Nothing would ever be the same. Would I see the boys grow up? Did John care? What happens when you die? How could I prepare? Would John love me with all my hair shaved off? Who would look after the boys? The questions went on endlessly tormenting me and circling round until I reached exhaustion and simply gave in and lay staring at the case on the chair, no more feelings, no more questions, and the whole room out of focus except for the bright yellow cover on the Bible, the one vivid colour in a white clinical nightmare.

One thing was clear in my mind. I was facing death. Whenever I have a problem in life I have always been organized and set up my plan. I knew that the thoughts confusing my mind needed to clear and I needed to face all the approaching issues and be able to prioritize. Much as I tried to apply this well-tested formula, however, the thoughts still poured into my mind in a dislocated way. I gave up trying and just let my mind wander. My thoughts went back to the start of the problem. I could remember exactly which day it began because it was a special day. It was Mayday and a time of great fun for the local community. Every Mayday a large funfair came to the park at the centre of our houses and with Mayday being a school holiday all the families gathered at the funfair, everyone smiling and laughing, carrying candy floss and goldfish and teddies won on the stalls. There were small rides for the children and people took picnics and sat chatting on the grass observing one another's pleasure. It was a day we all looked forward to except for me. I pretended to be excited for the boys' benefit but the day just emphasized an unhappiness in my life. I was very aware that our family seemed dislocated. John's job was demanding and took up ever-increasing amounts of his time as he progressed up the ladder of success. He loved the boys but had little time for them and I felt that our family was low on his priority list. This was not as I had imagined our lives would become. To be with him and share a family life was all I really wanted, not being academic or ambitious, and I was dissatisfied. As John's work opened up opportunities for him to work in America, I was sometimes left alone with Charlie and Sam for periods of time and, not being maternal, I found those times exhausting and once the boys were in bed I faced an aching loneliness. Also, John had a hobby involving his love of mathematics, puzzles, and his creativity and this filled his spare time. It verged on an obsession from which we were more or less excluded. I had never been a sporty person and John loved squash so other parts of his spare time were used for this and I was never comfortable with him enjoying sport with other women, particularly women from work. In my insecurity I felt very vulnerable and responsible for Charlie and Sam. I felt as if my time had of necessity to be meeting their needs and that I was not as attractive to John as these women because I could not give him what they did. I felt ugly alongside them as I had little money to spend on fashion and little time to spend on my appearance. I felt that my marriage was being threatened by circumstances beyond my control and this was not how I wanted our lives to be. The Mayday fair summed up all my unhappiness as John's work prevented him from coming with us.

I prepared a picnic for us as two excited figures bounced up and down and put on my act of sharing how they saw the day. As we made our way across the woods to the park, the noise of the fairground rides and laughter became nearer as we approached. Everyone seemed to be united as families and united as a community. All the children had their Daddies. Maybe there were others like me but I felt so alone and deserted but determined that my feelings would not prevent Charlie and Sam from having the time of their lives. They laughed as they rode on ladybirds and swung on swings. We ate hot dogs and ice cream and tired but happy they walked back with me across the woods carrying the big blue bear that they had won. For them it was a lovely day but for me I felt sad and exhausted and was beginning to feel a headache coming on. I only ever had headaches if I had a high temperature, and I was very rarely ill so this was unusual. By the time we arrived home it was getting worse and unusual for me. I took a couple of paracetamol before I bathed the children and put them to bed. I read them a story and tucked them up and tired and happy they and the blue bear were soon asleep. As I rested in the evening, the headache was becoming unbearable and the tablets were having no effect so I poured myself a large glass of whisky and went to bed.

I was woken in the morning by two bouncy boys ready for a new day, and as I surfaced from sleep I was aware that all was not well. Thankfully, the excruciating headache had gone but I was left with a burning stabbing in my right eye, aching in my ear, raging toothache, and pain all down the side of my face. I shovelled down paracetamol and fed Weetabix to hungry mouths. I was concerned about the pain as the following weekend was my brother's wedding and I knew I had to pack for us and travel 300 miles. I loved my brother so much and I had been so looking forward to the weekend away and some time with John and my family. Knowing my family, there would be a lot of delicious food, a lot of drinks and fun, and I wanted to enjoy it. Thankfully for me, the pain eased as the week progressed and by the time I was packing to go I was tired but pain free and ready to enjoy the weekend of a lifetime. Little did I know it would return with a vengeance in a few months time!

Entertaining two small people on a long journey took a lot of doing and we arrived at the hotel tired but very happy. Already friends and family were gathering and we had an evening ahead of us to enjoy before the wedding on Saturday. Two chocolate-covered boys were washed and put to bed and we launched into exactly what I had expected, fun, food, and drink. We were all so happy and excited.

In the morning I explained to Charlie and Sam what was to happen that day and how special it was. Thinking that a church service would be boring and long for them and knowing that the reception would seem endless, we had invited a lovely lady, Mary, who lived near us and who regularly babysat for us. We planned that they should go out for the day and then return to be cleaned and smartened for a small part of the reception so that they were included in the celebrations. Dressed happily in old clothes they set off for a short train journey, a real treat for them, to a fun-filled day on the beach enhanced by ice cream. Once they were hugged goodbye, I returned to our hotel room to get dressed, free for a short while of my responsibilities and with a little time for myself. I would never class myself as glamorous and I do not have the face or figure of a model but dressed in an outfit that I liked I felt that I had done my best for my brother and I felt good. I was so happy for him and I looked forward to a day when I was not just "a mum."

As we approached the church, people were gathering outside and there was a buzz of anticipation. My father was behaving in his usual entertaining way, wearing my mother's hat for the photographer and teasing her in front of friends. My brother wore his usual beaming smile and tears came into my eyes as I thought how much this day meant to him. Once inside the church the atmosphere changed to a more serious note as Jim stood at the front waiting for his bride. The sight of her took my breath away. A petite and pretty girl with long hair, she had an ability to wear her hair up and instantly transform herself into elegance. Today, she looked stunning and radiant; a dress that would have looked silly and fussy on me made her tiny figure so feminine and her expression said "I feel wonderful and this is the best day of my life."

Through tears I watched as they made their vows knowing that Jim meant every word. Tears of joy for them were mixed with tears of aching sorrow for us.

I remember thinking, "Please don't let their marriage end up like ours." I thought of our wedding day when I was only too aware that a four-year engagement had robbed us of the spontaneous feelings of romantic love and I had walked up the aisle wearing a boil on my chin, the size of a two-penny coin. It was an act of will and commitment to make legal, before God and men, a heart commitment I had made four years before. There was a surface joy but a pain inside. I did love John but we have realized since that love does not always depend on gooey feelings but there was now no romance or fun. It was all hard work with me seeming to do the bulk of it. It had become broken nights, evenings apart while I babysat, endless chores, resentment, and nappy buckets. The time given to Charlie and Sam took my freedom away to enjoy time with John and he seemed not to feel a need to be with me. I had become his domestic help cum mother rather than someone he was in love with. I felt bored, exhausted, lonely, rejected, insecure, and afraid, threatened by other women and deeply concerned for our future as a family.

After the wedding, we returned to the hotel where Charlie and Sam appeared having been cleaned up by Mary. We all enjoyed the reception and Charlie's moment of glory came when, aided by a family friend, he put a coin in a fruit machine and won the jackpot! His eyes shone as he crawled on the floor collecting coins as more rained on his head from above!

That night, trying to dismiss fear of the future, I cuddled into bed beside John only too aware of the distance between us. Where were we going and what on earth would happen to us and the boys? I wondered if John felt as miserable as I did but concluded that he never even thought about it but distracted himself with work and hobbies whereas I was forced to recognize the depths to which we had plummeted. I was glad the following day to be home and get on with life.

Memories of the wedding moved through my mind as if I was turning the pages of an album until I was suddenly propelled into the present and jolted into the reality of my hospital room. It was so cold and clinical and I longed to be home. I desperately wanted to leave but could not. Whatever was to come I had to make a plan, but where should I start? I surveyed the white walls as if expecting some written instructions to appear on them. There was a nothingness about the whole scene and certainly no plan! I chose to give up planning and decided to rest and recover from the trauma of the day. I was very tired.

As I closed my eyes and shut out the whiteness of the room, the last thing I saw was the bright yellow rectangle shouting at me from inside my case – the well-used Bible. I lay with my eyes closed and my mind went back to how I had come to possess it and the fascinating man to whom it meant so much.

Chapter 2

The Most Expensive Gift

John's hobbies brought him into contact with many people from all different walks of life and it was them that I was interested in. I knew John derived a lot of satisfaction from what he did but I was a musician and found the puzzles and mathematics boring. However, I enjoyed meeting the people and always liked it when they came to stay.

One weekend John suggested that we should invite a member from Scotland down to share some time together. I was told that he was a minister in the Church of Scotland and so I was not too sure if I would feel comfortable with him. John reassured me that I would find him a very pleasant visitor and seemed very eager to see him again and so I agreed and Robert was invited to stay. I was totally unprepared for the person I was about to meet.

I imagined he would arrive wearing a dog collar and carrying a briefcase, and realizing that he would have experienced an eight-hour journey, I knew he would be tired and organized the boys so that they would give him time to have a rest. We were all ready when the doorbell rang. Like a cork out of a champagne bottle in bounded about six feet of high energy. As soon as he saw the boys he said "look what I've got," and reaching into his pockets proceeded to pull out three juggling balls. Kneeling on the hall floor to our amazement he proceeded to juggle the balls and catch them on his back. Charlie and Sam became just as hyperactive and forgetting to be quiet they joined in his entertainment with great enthusiasm. How could he have such energy? Who was the tigger that had come to stay? Everything about him spoke of joy and a great love of life. He enjoyed the minutest details, his eyes sparkling, and a constantly happy smile. Once we had eaten and the boys had gone to bed, I decided to observe this man more closely as he and John enthused about their hobby. To outwards appearances Robert had very little concern about appearance. His trousers were old as was his shirt and I could see that a little mending would not have come amiss. His standards were obviously very different from mine. I liked to keep reasonably up to date with fashion and was concerned with my appearance, which never reached satisfaction. The expected dog collar was not there and the briefcase was a supermarket bag containing very little. In fact, I wondered what he would be wearing for the weekend, but he seemed far more interested in enjoying himself than worrying about that. If he was tired he never showed it and eagerly helped me with the washing up, something John never did! As we worked together, he talked enthusiastically about so many subjects. He also asked me about myself, with his sparkling eyes changing to a look of loving concern for my needs. I could see that below the surface energy lay a deep seriousness and concern for others that was confirmed by his tale of meeting a down and out and spending his bus fare on buying the man a drink and meal. The tale was told with no boasting but a great concern for that man's needs and for his future. Yes, I concluded, Robert was different. If I wanted to

be snobby I would say he was poor but I could see that he
had a richness that was missing in my life, a peace that was
not mine, and a joy. Because he was a church minister I felt
that I should try to find something in common with him
and so I told him I knew a few Christians at the Methodist
church where I took the boys to a toddler group and Sunday school. I did not tell him that I used this as a babysitting
service and a breather from the exhaustion of two small
bundles of energy. He told me he knew Jesus and what a
wonderful God he had got. I did not take too much notice of
what he said but two things stayed in my mind. He said that
it had recently been one of his greatest joys to travel several
hundred miles in a white minibus with a group of young
Christians singing praises to Jesus all the way.

"How boring!" was my silent comment. The other thing
he said was that Jesus always gave him enough for himself
and something to give to others. I remember thinking

"You're so poor you couldn't give me anything." We
spent a crazy weekend with two hyperactive boys and one
six-foot-tall hyperactive vicar! He was certainly the most
unusual and fascinating man I had ever met and I could not
help contrasting my unhappiness with his joy and wonder
about my mundane misery and exhaustion.

John took Robert to the station and I watched him carrying his bag with so little in it and I thought, "There you
are. You were wrong; you had nothing left over to give
to me." On returning home, John and I talked about the
weekend and as John enthused about his hobby I grew
bored and tired and suggested we get an early night. As
we got into bed I felt that the bedclothes had been dis-
turbed in some way and as I slid my feet down the bed
they reached something cold, hard, and rectangular. Puzzled by this I thought "this is Robert, he has left something." As my feet examined the object my mind became

wildly excited at the thought of a box of chocolates ...
how kind! I pulled the object up the bed and transferred it
from my feet to my hands and into the light. Yes, he had
left me something, his Bible as colourful as the man who
had given it and who obviously had read it many times
and to whom it meant so much. Unimportant then, now
facing death it was possibly becoming more important
to me.

I lay smiling as I remembered Robert and the peace and
joy he radiated, then suddenly I was transported into the
present and the shock of my situation. Looking back was
not going to solve my problem. I had to look forward,
prioritize, and make a plan. I always thought it was natural
for a mother to put her children first but I found that in
this crisis it was not so. Perhaps I am unnatural, perhaps I
am a poor mother but facing death my first thoughts were
for me. Where was I going? What would happen to me?
Would it be painful? What would I see as I closed my eyes
for the last time? It was no comfort or consolation that one
day everyone has to die and that so many billions of people
had gone this way before me. It was similar to childbirth.
Even though every person who has been born had a mother
who had been through this, it did not take away my fear of
the unknown and of pain. I looked at the Bible cover and
thought. I could not believe that I was going into oblivion.
There seemed no sense to me having spent thirty years in
this amazing world and shared them with so many people
that I would just disappear. I believed there had to be something after death. I could also not believe that this wonderful world, so immaculately made and so detailed beyond
what man can create, could just be here and just happen. I
did believe that there was a superior creator and so I suppose I did believe in God. I could see no useful purpose in
religion that gave people rules to live by and restrictions

that created limitations and habits. If there was a God, did he really create us to enclose us in a narrow box for his benefit? My answer had to be "no." Did the Bible matter? It obviously did to Robert and to read it was his priority, it seemed. However, people of other religions had holy books that were different so why should the Bible contain truth and not the books they had? If there was a God, and I concluded there had to be, how could a person find him? Could he be found? If I prayed would he listen? What was he like? So many questions that had never seemed important in all my thirty years now were very important. If he was there I needed him now, not just for my present but my future. How could I find him? Where should I start?

I had one clue and it came from my son Charlie. My pregnancy with him was not straightforward and he was born with many physical difficulties, which we knew over the years we would have to sort out. About a year before I became ill, we had to take little Charlie to the ear, nose, and throat hospital for an operation. I sat with him the night before we were to go and showed him the case I had packed for him, with new pyjamas and a wash bag with happy faces on. I looked with a pain in my heart as I observed his childish trusting excitement as he emptied the contents of the wash bag and admired his new toothbrush. For him it was an adventure, but I knew it meant pain. I gently told him all about hospitals. In fact, I had been preparing him for weeks. I explained that he would go to sleep and that while he was asleep the doctors would make his nose better and that when he woke up it would hurt for a while as it healed. He was a very placid child and accepted this with his usual steadiness, but then he came across something he could not cope with. Because he was first on the operating list, I had to starve him overnight and he could not have any breakfast. This he was not

happy about and he made that fact very clear. Protesting
his hunger I took him early to the hospital and with the
help of some wonderful thoughtful nurses settled him into
his bed. We covered again clearly what was to happen,
but he was not interested. He wanted breakfast! He was
wheeled off to the theatre complaining and I sat to await
his return. The kindly nurse gave me a cup of tea to help
pass the time and I spent the time watching the activity of
the ward and the unfamiliar surroundings. As Charlie was
only having a small operation, it was not too long before a
still little figure was brought back to the ward and placed
beside me, looking a little pale and sleepy beneath a clean
white sheet. As he turned over I reached to stroke his face.
He opened his eyes and looked at me and said "Don't
worry about me. I've had my breakfast with a little boy
whose Daddy is a carpenter!" What a strange thing to say!
He then went back to sleep leaving me pondering. I could
only think of one little boy whose Daddy was a carpenter
... Jesus .... but did Charlie know anything about this?
When he woke up I asked him how he felt, and typically
of Charlie, he accepted the pain and lay still. "What is a
carpenter?" I asked him.

"I don't know," he replied. I repeated to him what he
had said but he could remember nothing. I could not get
his words out of my mind and decided to tell someone
about it. The person I knew would have an opinion was
my grandmother. I knew she went to church and as a child
I had watched her kneel by her bed to pray. I remembered
one day sleeping in her bed at her bungalow and snuggling
beside her as she read her Bible. I told her what Charlie
had said and as I had expected, she gave me a direct honest
reply.

"If he said he did then he did! Don't you dare to cause
him to doubt!"

I never understood what Charlie had experienced that day or why, but I had always carried the memory in my mind and now it was becoming more important. He said he did ... so did he? If it was so, how wonderful! But could something so wonderful be true. Here was my starting point and my priority ... to prove to myself whether Jesus is God and if so was he alive and could he hear our prayers and intervene in our lives? I was so desperate and frightened and I might not have long, so my first step in my plan was to start praying and see what happened.

But how do you pray? I had been to church and hated it. The reciting of prayers seemed artificial and impersonal. If there was a God, I wanted one I could be myself with, so I decided to start in a small way.

I'm frightened and in trouble so if you're there please help," was my honest prayer. There was no answer. A nurse came into the room with a cheery smile followed by a young man in a white coat.

"We're just going to take some blood," she announced. I was well used to this as I had a rhesus negative blood group and so during my pregnancies had had many needles stuck in me. I felt OK with this and hoped it would provide some useful information. One or two jabs of a needle were so minor in comparison with the burning stabbing in my face. After about ten jabs, they left with several files of blood and then I was ushered into a small room rather resembling that of an optician with no windows and a lot of apparatus. A nurse started sticking electrodes all over my head with glue. This was unknown territory for me and it seemed like a bad dream. Needing to know facts I asked hundreds of questions, all of which were patiently answered and I found the tests I had to do quite challenging because it was difficult to concentrate on their instructions with the enormity of pain in my head. Once it was over, I was escorted back to my room and found I was becoming less concerned and unnerved by patients walking in the corridors with shaved heads and drips and metal frames. "Maybe it won't be so bad," I hoped but I did not know what was to come after lunch.

A couple of doctors arrived and sat on my bed. "We've studied your case history," they announced in a matter of fact way, "and we have a suspicion that this might be multiple sclerosis and so we need to do a lumbar puncture."

The words "lumbar puncture" had the confusing effect of making me want to run through the door as fast as I could yet at the same time hide under the bed! I had a friend who had undergone a lumbar puncture and at the time I had mentally logged it in the section of my brain containing things that I would rather die than cope with. But much as I wanted to, there was no escape. The only way was through this and I had never been so petrified in my life! I was told to lie on my side on a clean white sheet and I shook all over. I shall never forget the doctor who performed the procedure. She had large brown eyes that looked kind and reassuring. I decided to confess my terror and she agreed that although she would be behind me she would tell me exactly what she was going to do in advance and little by little she guided me through it. She reassured me that she did this everyday and I was surprised by how little it hurt. The fear far outweighed the pain as was confirmed by the pool of sweat that was left where I had lain. Did God hear my prayer? Was he helping? Well maybe he sends people of compassion to comfort terrified people but the help I needed was far more than that.

In my room the next morning there was a happy start to the day. My gentle aunt Sylvia arrived bringing an enormous bunch of flowers. I was so touched that she had given her time to come and also I knew that it was hard for her to afford them. Her life in recent years had been one of suffering having been widowed at an early age because of cancer. Out of her suffering she had learnt sensitivity and I loved her for her kindness and understanding. As she sat silently on the side of my bed her eyes filled with tears and I could see all her pain mixed with mine. Her tears said more than words and showed such love. Sometimes saying nothing says so much. She did not stay long because a nurse came and politely ushered her out as the sounds of busy scuffling rose up behind the door.

In walked "the Prof" followed by a couple of junior doctors who stood each side of my bed. "We are gradually getting a picture of what is going on," he explained. "Scans and X rays have shown there is no brain tumour and we do not think this is multiple sclerosis. You have borderline failed one of the tests but the lumbar puncture is clear so we are confident that MS is not the problem." I felt such relief but foolishly because I did not want John to see me with my head shaved; but relief soon turned again to frustration. What was this unbearable pain in my head that overrode all my thinking and exhausted me with pent up screams?

"I think this is vascular," announced one of the junior doctors over my bed to his colleague who nodded. I hadn't a clue what he meant. "We need to investigate for an aneurysm, an enlargement of an artery which could be fatal if it bursts," continued "the Prof" in an everyday way. "To do this we need to do an angiogram," he continued explaining that they would pass a tube up a blood vessel in my arm up to my brain and then inject dye to highlight any abnormalities. "We can do this with a local anaesthetic or a general. Which would you prefer?" With my lifelong fear of pain and the increasing terror I gratefully requested a general and the nodding-dog doctors and the team all agreed and left the room to make arrangements. The pain was unbearable but at least the knowledge that I would be asleep was welcome.

Nurses prepared me again and I remember nothing until I woke up. Initially I felt excruciating pain through a haze of doziness and gradually my senses returned. I looked around the room to get my bearings. There was the table, the door, and my case. I turned over and felt dizzy and looked at the window. There was the window frame but I could not see the car park! It was a complete misty blur. I double checked that I could see the room but I could see nothing in the distance of the car park or the trees! I was not aware of being warned of any dangers in what was being done and had the sinking feeling that the angiogram had damaged my sight. Before I had time to really worry the door opened and in walked my father, his stethoscope around his neck (a very effective way of entering a hospital out of visiting hours). I was extremely surprised to see him, his work was so busy. I felt safe. With him there had always been security and safety. The soft stubby hands that had comforted so many were now comforting me. His words were positive and reassuring although I could detect an abruptness in his voice that he reserved for times when he was very concerned. I told him that I was very worried that I could not see in the distance. I was going blind so why on earth was he laughing? It was not at all amusing and did not make sense until he explained that he had had great difficulty in driving as there was a really thick fog that day and he too could not see the car park! We laughed together ... such relief.

When the results of the angiogram came through "the Prof" returned and said I could go home. My life was not in danger, it was all clear. I was desperate to go home but this left me in exactly the same situation as I had been originally except that I had lived through days of pain and terror beyond my imagining. "We may never know what caused this "the Prof" concluded "but you cannot live with this degree of pain. We have decided to sever the nerve on the right side of your face so it will be numb. You will not be able to close your eyes and your lip will be numb. You will have to keep shampoo out of your eyes but you will soon get used to all this. It is the best option." I was so desperate to be out of pain I would have agreed to anything in order to make a happy Christmas for Charlie and Sam but I knew there was a cost to this that the "Prof" was unaware of. I am an oboist playing a woodwind instrument in an orchestra. This was my profession and my greatest pleasure before I had a family and with no feeling in my lips it would be the end of my career. Still I had no choice. I agreed to go ahead with the procedure but horror returned with a vengeance as it was explained to me that it would have to be done without an anaesthetic as they needed me to be awake and feeling in order to tell them when the pain was numb. This was explained to me as if it was something that happened to everyone everyday. Were they totally unaware of how terrifying a prospect this was to me? Why was I being asked to face things beyond my ability to bear? There was no way out unless there was God and he was doing nothing. He was a dead loss, I felt hopelessly. "The Prof" made arrangements for the day of my torture next Friday and discharged me numb with shock to return home to catch up on the washing and make arrangements for the following week.

However, before I had gathered up my belongings the door opened again and there stood the vicar from the church where I dumped the boys. Having heard of my situation from one of the girls in the toddler group he had come to offer what help he could. I appreciated his time, knowing he was as busy as my father, and thought he had a kind heart. He sat on the bed and having asked what was going on he did what he could to comfort. "Something will come along to replace your oboe playing, he offered kindly, and I'm sure you will soon learn to eat again." His words meant to comfort hit me again with another blow. It had never occurred to me that I would have trouble eating and swallowing. This was all sheer nightmares from which I could not wake up. The vicar said the church would pray for me about which I felt extremely embarrassed and I resisted the temptation to tell him that I was not mightily impressed with God so far!

If there was a God he did not seem to be on my side and he certainly seemed to be very distant and inactive. I asked the vicar to thank the ladies of the church who had been wonderfully supportive of John in a practical way. They had organized rotas for collecting and looking after the boys, had cooked casseroles and done all they could to help. I was so grateful to them. We could not have managed without them.

Chapter 3

Six Weeks to Christmas

Having said goodbye to the vicar and phoned John, I packed my case to return home with the intention of restoring order to chaos and security for Charlie and Sam, and also to prepare for what I had to face. I decided to concentrate on the fact that it was six weeks to Christmas and by then it would all be over and I would be out of pain. I needed a plan and the plan was to reassure, organize, prepare, and secure the boys and to get everything in order at home. I was an immaculate perfectionist, home was tidy and clean. John was not at all domesticated and I dreaded what I would return to.

I was right. To my perfectionist eyes the house was like a bombsite. Books, toys, and papers were everywhere. There were piles of washing and washing up, enough work to keep me busy for a week and distract me from what was to come. I had to keep putting the fear to the back of my mind and look outwardly calm so that Charlie and Sam would not be upset. Tidying, cleaning, and washing were regularly interrupted by wiping dirty faces, giving cuddles, refereeing fights, and telling stories. Among the stories was the true story of Mummy going back to hospital for the doctors to make her better. Oh that it had been that simple!

John was not impressed by the timing of the whole thing. It coincided with the Christmas disco for his firm's employees and he was planning to go with Sarah, a secretary with whom he regularly played squash. Sarah was a happy person who was always very pleasant to me and I knew their friendship was platonic but I was still very uncomfortable and threatened by it. Here was a very attractive woman, not worn out by children, not associated with the mundane hassles of family life who could share John's love of sport. This made me feel very insecure and I hated the firm's rules that husbands and wives were not allowed at the social events. I felt like an unpaid babysitter and when sharing how I felt with a close friend was not at all helped when she said her husband would not dream of going without her. Pete, Sarah's husband, seemed without me saying to understand. He seemed to know how alone I felt when John went out and he often came and spent the evening with me. I enjoyed being with Pete because I could have in-depth conversations with him that John would not have considered. Pete was a deep thinker, asking similar questions about life as I was. We talked for hours while Sarah and John danced and the boys slept. We ate vindaloo curries and drank more whisky than was good for us. Sometimes we played dominoes. Pete was a great comfort to me. He made me feel I had value. One night while John and Sarah were at a firm's do we talked about the possibility of God and Pete mentioned Christians and his comment was "I hope for them they are right because they pay such a high cost." It was something I had never considered but I know now that in his journey through life Pete had found a truth that I had missed. If only I had known the cost. Perhaps it is best that I did not.

When the dreaded evening arrived on Thursday I kissed the boys and set off with John and Sarah to the hospital, terror turning into unreality. Pete stood in the porch with two little figures holding each of his hands and waving. I felt utterly miserable. It was easy for John. He was going to a disco. Did he not realize what I was facing? Could he not hear what I was saying? I needed him but he chose to go to a disco as if nothing was happening. Was that how much he loved me? It did not seem as if life was worth living and yet there were two small boys to look after and who needed me. I had to go through this for them.

John and I said goodbye in my hospital room and I unpacked my belongings. The teddy, yes, the Bible, no! It did not help, it was all irrelevant and a waste of time. However, I still thought that a plaintive cry to a possible God would be at the least a few seconds of breath and so as I settled down in my bed trying to contain so many emotions I prayed a quick "If you're there please do what's best for me."

The time for the operation came faster than I had expected. A nurse came to prepare me giving me an injection and a theatre gown and I was taken on a trolley to the operating theatre. I kept concentrating on how severe the pain was and tried to persuade myself that it would be worth this to be out of pain at Christmas. The wait outside the theatre seemed endless and then an orderly came to wheel me in, or so I thought. To my astonishment, he turned me round and moved back in the direction we had come and took me back to my room.

"What's going on?" I asked.

'You can go home!" he replied "There's been a major traffic accident and we need all the theatres. You can come back after the weekend on Monday!"

I felt as if I was going to explode and burst apart, throwing all the repressed emotions all over the room, but what exploded was an anger of the enormity I had never experienced. I was absolutely furious and it was God who got the brunt of my anger. Did not he realize how I had had to gear myself up for the ordeal, did not he realize the fear, did not he know I wanted to be out of pain for Christmas and that I had a lot to do to get ready and buy presents? I had asked him to do the best for me and what he had done was the worst! It is amazing how furious you can be with a God you do not believe in!

John came to fetch me later that day to wait another tormenting weekend in which I alternated washing the boys with trying to keep them and myself calm and with stroking the blue velvety furry case of my oboe as if saying goodbye to it forever. Throughout the weekend the pain in my right eye and ear continued to stab and burn and I numbed it with whisky to push down the screams and drink myself into oblivion to escape. I was unprepared for Sunday morning and the major change that was to occur in my situation. All the pain on the right side had gone! Was it a miracle? No. It had completely moved to the left side of my face and was attacking me there. Well, they say a change is as good as a rest!

When I returned to the neurosurgical hospital, as they prepared me for theatre, I informed them of the change and commented lightly that as they were severing the nerve on the right side of my face they would have to do the same to the one on my left. The nodding-dog doctor looked puzzled and thoughtful and disappeared to consult "the Prof" with whom he returned. "I have cancelled your operation," he said calmly.

"As the pain has moved, to do this would be inappropriate." I was so relieved but so puzzled as he made arrangements for me to rest and consult him the next day.

As I sat opposite him looking across his large wooden desk I detected a look of concern and he spoke with compassion. I did not see the stern strict man who held his staff in fear. "I have no idea what is causing your pain," he concluded. "This happens in many cases. All I can say is that your life is not in danger. Your pain is severe but there is nothing that can be done. I do hope for you that it will go away as mysteriously as it came and that until it does you will be able to find a way to live with it. Please give my regards to your father. I will write to him."

I thanked him and said goodbye and walked outside with my little case to catch the bus home. I had been through trauma that was unimaginable and terror I had never known, facing things I could not have faced and now I was left exhausted, shocked, and in the same unbearable situation I had been in when I first arrived at the hospital, still in pain. Pondering on all of this on the bus I realized that the operation would have been a catastrophic mistake for me. I would have lost the feeling in half of my face and the movement and my career and joy in music only to be in just as much pain again. I had to acknowledge that God had done the best for me. When I looked back I could see it. The traffic accident, the cancellation, the wait were all necessary. Was it just coincidence or was it a God who could see a far bigger picture than I could?

Chapter 4

Finding the Way

I decided to put the trauma of the last few weeks behind me and to concentrate on moving forwards and so as I made my way home on the bus, I made up my plan. The plan was to catch up on and organize Christmas and to try and find a way to live with the pain. Perhaps it would just go away. I could always hope. Being a very organized person and in control, by now I would have been way ahead in my preparations with presents bought, cards written, and meals planned in plenty of time. I had only to be jumped upon by two highly excited boys to realize that they and everyone else was way ahead of me. The rush would be good for me in distracting me from the pain but I really did feel too ill for doing all this, although the two eager faces lit up with anticipation spurred me on to effort and I launched into a frantic burst of shopping, making lists and bedtime stories.

John had to go and work in America for two weeks before Christmas and I hated that. I was not the maternal kind and the demands of being on duty twenty-four hours a day exhausted, frustrated and left me washed out at the best of times. Now with Christmas near, I needed him with me but I knew he had to go. Once he had left, I moved up a gear to push through the endless lists of things to do and alternated activity with a glass of whisky to help comfort the pain. When I was exhausted from pain I moved the sleeping Sam into my bed to remind me that there was a reason to keep going and to cuddle. Suicide was not an option.

On the day that John arrived home the pain had squeezed me to pieces but I did not want to tell him how bad it had been. I went upstairs and selected my favourite black dress and shoes, dressed up as well as I could, washed my hair, and put on some makeup and perfume to greet him. I breathed a sigh of relief as I heard the key in the door and stood up to hold out my arms to a very tired looking man. It had obviously been a very draining trip. It was quiet without the boys in the house in the afternoon and we sat side by side on the settee holding hands and saying little. Words could not say how hard I had found it without him and I did not want to moan. He was too tired to talk so we just sat until John made an unusual comment. "You've got all dressed up just for me." I was glad that he had noticed and appreciated the effort it had taken. However, it did raise a worrying thought in my mind. He had been away on his own for two weeks. "I'm sorry, John," I whispered in his ear as I lay to one side against him. "I'm in so much pain that I can't face" ..... My words were interrupted by a gentle "It's OK. I'm not feeling too much like it myself. I'll go and fetch Charlie and Sam if you like so you can have a rest." I was so grateful for that understanding.

About an hour later, in burst two whirling bundles of pre-Christmas excitement, hurling hand painted calendars and cards and teacher's letters and lunch boxes, scattering duffle coats and elasticated mittens everywhere. Daddy was home! Christmas was coming! Christmas was magical for children, it always was for me at home and I loved to observe their joy. The elves were coming to put up decorations as they slept and chocolate was in abundance! What a shame we have to grow up!

With the boys tucked up in bed, we sat in peaceful silence and I sipped whisky until I became sleepy and we decided to make it an early night. It was so comforting to snuggle up next to John knowing he was as tired as I was. It had been a difficult time.

As the countdown to Christmas continued I grew increasingly perplexed by John's lack of interest in it all. Could he not see all the effort I was making for him and the boys? I felt as if I was doing all the work and through the pain putting on an act of excitement for the boys while he was distancing himself from it all. It did not feel like being a family. I concluded that the trip abroad had taken it out of him and that he needed to relax and see the fun of it all and so in order to share it, I planned to save wrapping Charlie and Sam's presents until they were in bed on Christmas eve and so involve John. We could do it together. I turned down the lights to emphasize the lights on the tree and poured two glasses of sherry, then I knelt down on the carpet and began to wrap a shiny black taxi for Sam. John sat and made no moves towards helping and I started to feel frustration mounting. In the end after another glass of sherry it blew. "What is the matter with you? If you do not want to be with us, why do not you just go and leave us to get on with this? The least you could do is to wrap a few gifts for your children. Go away and leave me to pretend by myself!"

HAPPY CHRISTMAS!!! We spent a silent two hours wrapping presents and then took the boys' pillow cases up to their room and slipped them beside their beds very quietly so as not to wake them. I drank a couple of glasses of whisky and lay down in bed back to back with John, silent tears streaming down my face. What had this illness done to us and where were we going? I felt an approaching doom.

Christmas passed and the boys had a wonderful time. I had the satisfaction of knowing that I had pulled it off and on December 31st we moved into a new year with a feeling of dread in my heart.

I went to see my father to see if there was a plan medically, but it seemed there was no hope. Because of the strange incident of the traffic accident, I had a small incentive to look in the Bible to see if there might be a clue and even though I am not a reader, I chose to have a little search from time to time. The problem was I could not understand it at all; it was totally irrelevant and meaningless. I could not understand why Robert, its owner, saw it as being of such value. What was the use of Jesus feeding the five thousand when you have got pain beyond belief! My father tried several drugs but even morphia would not relieve the pain. It just made me muzzy and unable to function. I just could not cope and I would bottle up the screams for a couple of days and then go absolutely berserk, hurling myself around the room and banging my head on the walls screaming. John perfected the art of following me around and predicting where I was going to be and then thrusting a cushion between my head and the wall to prevent me from hurting myself. I realized that I could only get through this if I could have a break from pain through sleep, but I found it impossible to sleep. This caused me to resort to a very self-destructive plan. I stayed sober all day to look after the boys, then as soon as John came in I drank whisky until I could feel sleep coming on and sank into oblivion. When I awoke the pain was still there and so we started another day, and that was how it went on. After a few months, I was getting through three bottles of whisky a week (which we could little afford) but I did not know any other way until one day I came up with an idea of investigating alternative medicine. I discussed it with John and my father who agreed to refer me to a well-respected doctor who practised acupuncture. We knew it would be expensive but we were desperate and it gave me hope as I booked my first appointment.

It was October when I set off for my first visit to Dr Burness. I remember it well for the freshness of the air and the crunch of leaves in the autumn sunshine. It reminded me so much of the night in October when I left our house and stood in golden leaves, their colour highlighted by the street light and I was helped into an ambulance. I relived the excitement I felt as I journeyed to hospital to give birth to Sam, eager to meet this little person I had been carrying around inside myself for nine months. This October I was excited too but this was because I had recaptured hope. Maybe acupuncture could get rid of my pain.

I drove up the cul de sac of expensive houses, parked, and nervously surveyed the outside of the house, not knowing why I was hesitating. I think I was afraid it would not work and I could not face lost hope. The door was opened by Dr Burness himself and it appeared that there was no one else in the house. The first impression of the house was how unusually silent it was except for the ticking of a large old clock. I did not like the ticking, it made me uncomfortable. Since I had been in pain I had found myself becoming increasingly intolerant of noise and I longed for quiet. This silence, however, was eerie. There was no hum of any electrical appliance and no sound of a bird song from the garden. Just the regular ticking of the clock.

Dr Burness ushered me upstairs to his consulting room and listened intently as I told him my tale of woe. He examined me and then exclaimed,

"Mrs Welton, I have never come across such a dreadful neck in all my life. If your father was here I could show him exactly what is wrong. No wonder you are in pain."

I was staggered. Here was someone who was claiming to know what was wrong. I was not going mad and imagining it. There was a reason.

"Do you think you can help me," I asked tentatively.

"Yes," he replied "It will take a few sessions but you will be *over the moon by Christmas.*" Goodness, here was another Christmas approaching and I had been through this for over a year and a half. He explained in detail and with confidence exactly what was going on and then began the acupuncture. Already in such pain I had not expected the needles to hurt and generally they did not, except it was nasty when they were pushed into the soft place at the side of my eyes. It was really strange. When the needles were taken out, it felt as if they were still there. After half an hour Dr Burness booked my next appointment for two weeks time by which time he said that today's session would have had its full effect. As I shook his hand I left with a beaming smile and a confident hope. This Christmas would be a happy one and last Christmas would disappear into the past.

During the following week, the acupuncture was definitely having an effect. The pain kept moving around and into my neck as Dr Burness had predicted and I was hopeful as I attended the next session. By the end of the sixth session, the pain was still there though with less of a headache, but I had developed the same stabbing pain in my pelvis and knees. Dr Burness seemed unperturbed by this, explaining that with acupuncture the problem goes back to its origin. He felt that a picture was building up and that all was going according to his plan. My problem was that again Christmas was coming and I was running out of money for the treatment. Kindly, my mother gave me enough money to continue and as John went off on another trip to America, I was undergoing another phenomenal effort to prepare again for the elves, Father Christmas, the washing of paint-covered nursery pinafores, and the wrapping paper, but at least the run up to this Christmas was not going to be interrupted by admissions to hospital. I shuddered as I remembered last year. As time went on though, despite Dr Burness's optimism I was coming to the realization that the pain was not going. It was just continually moving around my body and constantly in my head. My hope was beginning to fade and depression was on the attack. As Christmas drew near, it was becoming clear that I was not going to be over the moon. The last time I went for acupuncture, I was feeling so desperate, and when I told Dr Burness he suggested that he tried some manipulation of my neck. I would have agreed to anything and so I relaxed as he jerked my neck backwards and sideways with a big crack. It was not pleasant but it did not hurt too much and I thanked him as I left his care.

After a week, the manipulation that he had done with the best of intentions had made the pain worse beyond belief. I did not think it was possible for it to get worse, but it obviously could. I felt drunk with pain and I could not think or see. I was sure I was not safe driving because it was impossible to concentrate. When John returned from America, I was in a terrible state and hit the whisky bottle as soon as I could. The Christmas that came was one that I went through on automatic pilot, anaesthetized with alcohol. I even resorted to drinking the cooking Kirsch!

My hope was gone. All I had left was to give a possible God another try. I was suicidal and if God was there he might just do something and if he did not I would be meeting him soon after my death or disappearing into blissful oblivion. Even though my maternal instinct was to survive for the boys, it had gone and I reasoned that I was in no fit state to look after them and they would be better with John and he would be happier to marry again.

It was dark as I sat pathetically on my bedroom carpet. The curtains were open as I could not be bothered to close them and I could look up into a velvety navy blue sky. I thought about my predicament. I had run out of plans. I had given up. In my right hand was a bottle of vodka and in my left, Robert's Bible. I read a little bit and as usual it was incomprehensible, irrelevant, and useless. I took a large swig of vodka and tried again. No good! As the vodka started to anaesthetize my body and my pain, reading became more difficult and I moved from vodka to Bible alternately until I gave up and just stared at the night sky, nothing left. It was as I looked up that I heard the voice. It said "when you are at your weakest I am at my strongest." It was so clear. Was this the deranged mind of a drunken woman? Was I going mad? Could it be God? I did not even care anymore.

The next morning as I surfaced from a drunken sleep into a sea of pain, I forced myself up and went automatically through the routines of the day. Duffle coats were done up and small hands were held as we walked up to school. An about turn and I was walking back the same way, making beds, washing up, loading washing machines, and working through endless chores. Suddenly, a thought struck me. HYPNOSIS! Why had not I thought of it before? It was obvious. If I could see a hypnotist he could tell me I could not feel pain and it would be gone. Excitedly, I phoned my father. He was extremely worried. He knew me inside out and knew my suicidal threats were for real. Even so he did not for some reason share my enthusiasm. However, he was desperate to keep his daughter alive for the sake of the grandsons of whom he thought the world, and as I continued to plead he said that he knew a doctor who was a hypnotherapist and that he would refer me. The doctor lived some miles away and John needed the car so I took a very expensive taxi ride. I had no idea that what was about to begin would turn out to be the most amazing time of my life so far.

I was welcomed into the house by a tall broad-shouldered man wearing a suit and tie. It was obvious that this was a very expensive house in a very desirable area with lots of trees and laurel hedges. Dr George shook my hand and talked of his association with my father in a reassuring way and then guided me to his consulting room. Sitting upright on a chair, he asked about my problem and said he would be able to help. He asked me to lie back on a black leather couch rather like that of a dentist. As it tipped back I looked up at the ceiling as he dimmed the lights.

"We can only make a start today" he explained. "I am going to teach you to relax." He told me to imagine myself in my favourite place and my mind went straight to Herm, a little island in the Channel Islands where we had had happy times with Charlie and Sam. As I fixed my mind on this, I was aware of feeling uncomfortable for some unknown reason. The discomfort and unease started to grow until I was feeling actually threatened as if by something unseen. I felt in danger of some sort although I could not work out why. Here was a trusted friend of my father who would do me no physical harm, wanting to help me, and yet I felt an irrational danger. I wanted to run out and get away as soon as possible and I was very relieved when the session was over and I could clamber back into the taxi. My next appointment was booked but I had no desire, pain or no pain, to go back. I was utterly perplexed and puzzled. I mentioned how I felt to John but he, being a very practical person, could not understand what I was trying to say. As I pondered about it in bed that night, such a strange outcome to the day. I had a feeling that this was something deeper than I could understand and that it might have something to do with the supernatural or God, but if God was there I did not expect him to threaten me. It all did not make sense. I felt as if I was hurtling towards something very big that was out of my control and beyond my comprehension.

Chapter 5

Out of My Hands

When Charlie and Sam were out the next day, the unease increased. I knew I needed to talk to someone, but whom? I considered the vicar who had visited me in hospital but had the gut feeling that he would not know what I meant. I then thought of the Anglican Church up the road that I had peeped in years ago, but I could not see that a man in black gowns who gave a sermon once a week would know. How would he explain the unseen threat? As I wondered what to do, I suddenly remembered Robert. He would know what I was on about or at least try to understand. I would tell him my whole story as he knew nothing of our problems. If anyone might know it might be him.

I sat and wrote a letter to Robert, detailing the whole story and ending by drawing a pair of scales equally balanced with my pain on one side and the unseen threat on the other. I explained my dilemma and asked if he had any opinions or advice for me. I wrote his address in Scotland on the envelope and sent it first class and posted it on my way home from collecting Charlie and Sam.

The following evening, a tired John was wallowing in a hot bubble bath when the phone rang. I was pottering around picking up small pairs of trousers and picked up the phone to hear that lovely Scottish accent that immediately made me feel calmed. I had expected Robert to write not phone. He said "yes" he did have answers and advice but that what I was asking was deep. He then stunned me by saying "I don't think I should help you over the phone. I think God wants me to come down and see you and I am planning to come straight away!"

How ludicrous! To come all the way from Scotland, a busy man making an eight-hour journey because he thought God wanted him to. "You can't do that" I protested "You can't afford the train fare."

"If God wants me to come he'll provide the train fare," replied Robert with quiet confidence "I'll continue to pray about it and I'll phone you when I've made arrangements."

"Who was that?" enquired John from his bath.

"It was Robert from Scotland," I answered.

"It would be nice to see him again," said John with a contented tone in his voice.

"He says he is coming to see us soon," I continued as panic rose. I told John about my letter concluding "It's ridiculous for him to come. Just think of the train fare."

"If he wants to come I'll pay his train fare," offered John, unaware of our conversation and totally oblivious to Robert's words of faith for his financial needs. Everything seemed to be moving very fast and yet at the same time slowing into minute detail in a contradictory way.

The following day was a busy one for me preparing for Charlie's birthday. I always liked to make a special occasion of everyone's birthdays and was intending to make a cake like a chocolate bear. I was not particularly pleased to be interrupted by the doorbell. On opening the door, I faced a man of about our age, who I had never seen before, holding a wrapped gift package. He introduced himself as Chris and said "I hope you don't mind but its Charlie's birthday and I've bought him a present. It's a kite actually"

I was confused "How do you know?" I asked.

"My son is in Charlie's class" he replied "and he told me."

Kindness like this was not something I was used to and it took me aback. I then did twenty years ago something that you would not dream of doing now. I invited him in for a cup of tea. I felt it was the least I could do to thank him for his thoughtfulness. We sat and chatted awkwardly about our sons and then he came to his point.

"We are Christians" he said nervously "We've been praying and we think Jesus is telling us you are in some kind of trouble. We don't want to intrude but if you'd like to talk we know Jesus can help you."

Well how right he was! Some sort of trouble was the understatement of the decade. I told him we did have a problem and about the pain but omitted the embarrassing details like the drinking and my unhappiness. That was too private. He said that if I would like to go to their house they would be willing to pray with me, and then he added something that was bizarre to me. He said they would only pray with John's permission because God had put husbands in authority over their wives and Jesus would definitely do something and that whatever he did would affect both of us so John needed to agree. He left his telephone number for me to contact him and departed leaving me with a kite and an increasing awareness that something was going on that was out of my control.

In the evening, Robert phoned and, having come to terms with him coming, I excitedly answered, looking forward to seeing him again and enjoying the refreshing that his presence brought. His words were so different from what I had expected. I expected specific train times and was already setting up a plan to move Charlie and Sam out of their room to give him a bed. Instead he said simply "I've been praying and Jesus has told me not to come. He has said that he has already sent someone."

The coincidence boggled my mind! It had to be Chris but how did Robert know? Could he hear God? Was God in control of all of this mess? I certainly was not and I was not used to having no say in what was going on! I told Robert about Chris's visit and he said it was good and right and to go ahead, and then his soft Scottish voice contentedly bade me goodbye as if nothing extraordinary was happening.

So, to pray or not to pray? That was the question. The very thought of it embarrassed me and it went against all my pride and independence to accept help, or even acknowledge that I needed it from other people let alone God. What should I do? I needed to live for Charlie and Sam, and if there was a sliver of hope, I felt that I owed it to them. There seemed to be no choice, it was try or die! I picked up the phone with very mixed feelings and asked Chris to arrange to pray for me.

The next day Chris arrived at our home bringing with him Derek. Derek was a graduate in chemistry and obviously had academic intelligence far above mine and he carried a gentle air of authority. I could see by Chris's responses to him that he was regarded as "the leader of the pack." This unusual duo had come, not to see me but to talk to John, and had brought with them much appreciated offerings of beer. What on earth was going on? This was far removed from religion or God as I understood it. When the subject changed to prayer, Derek became very serious, as if he meant business. He explained to John that

God had put him in authority over his household (news to him!) and that they would pray for me only with his permission. John valued that but his response was "You can pray but don't expect me to get excited about it. I have seen hopes raised before and when it crashes I will be the one who has to pick up the pieces." They promised him their support and having drunk all the beer, they left but before doing so arranged for me to visit Derek's house the next day.

As I walked past the semi-detached houses where we lived to the smaller terraced houses where Derek lived, I felt very curious, as if I was heading towards an unknown with no choice in the matter. The pain in my head was excruciating and I longed for a cup of tea to warm it. Derek and his wife welcomed me into the house that was so different from mine. Being very materialistic, mine was newly decorated with the latest fashions and immaculately tidy. Here was a muddle of toys, washing on the stairs and an endless load of books. "If this is how God wants us to live," I thought, "he can keep it!" I had to recognize though that they were happy and not in the mess I was in. Derek's wife Trish made me the longed for mug of tea and I promised myself a double whisky when I got home.

Derek sat on a chair with his Bible and I sat politely on a bean bag as he started to explain what they were going to do. I felt so sorry for him as he read from the Bible. Out of kindness and concern, he was giving me his precious time and doing his best but he might as well have been reading Japanese as far as I was concerned. I could understand nothing! I did however understand when he put it in his own words that God wanted people to have a relationship with him and to know him (which was what I would have wanted if there was a God). This was prevented, he explained, by their sin. He told me that I, like everyone else, was a sinner (how dare he!) and needed to confess my sins and said that this would be part of what would need to happen. WHAT!! Do that in front of strangers! Oh no!! I felt humiliated, embarrassed, and puzzled.

"Do you know of any sins in your life?" He asked without appearing to judge or condemn.

"I'm not sure what sins are," was my answer. I had never even thought about it.

"Well have you done anything that would hurt God or go against what is in the Bible?" he continued.

I thought hard. I roughly knew the Ten Commandments from scripture lessons at school but I had honestly tried to be a good person. I might have told a few lies and there was the drinking, which I hated myself for but apart from that I had tried to be an obedient child, a good wife, and mother and done my best. However, Derek knew more about the Bible than me so I asked "Give me a clue."

"For a start, there is the acupuncture and the hypnotherapy," he replied. (So that was why I had felt so threatened) but his other suggestions surprised me. He asked if I read horoscopes, which I did, and did I wear a horoscope sign. He said I would need to bring it to the prayer night. He asked if I had been to a fortune teller or a séance and again the answer was yes. I did not know that God had a problem with that. If it was so important, why were we not told this in church? Derek talked about the devil opposing Jesus and a spiritual battle which had never crossed my mind. To me, the devil was a cute red toy with horns that was in the shops on Valentine's Day. To Derek, he was a very powerful spiritual being and enemy and I soon began to get the picture that this was not just about hymns, sermons and prayers, and rules and rituals. Christianity was about a spiritual battle that somehow I had got caught up in.

Derek told me to go home and, in a way, spring clean my house and put anything in a bag that offended God and to bring it to Chris's house the next evening. I thanked them for their time and kindness and they prayed for my protection. This was serious. I went home for my promised whisky and to begin my spring clean. Armed with a supermarket bag, I loaded it with my lovely Libran necklace, a load of books about horror stories and the occult, and then was unsure what else there could be. When I reached the little study, as I was passing the bookshelf my pranayama yoga handbook caught my eye. Was that OK? I decided to bag it as I could remember a vague feeling of threat, similar to that at the hypnotherapists. John and I had done yoga to relieve stress but it had done me no good. In fact, I hated John flirting with a girl in the class as I was getting increasingly larger with Sam's pregnancy and we left. One other thing that came to my mind was that John and I had slept together before we were married. I was not promiscuous and he was the first and only one. The night that we made love I committed myself to him exclusively for life in my heart. My parents always taught me that this was wrong, but their opinion, now that I was an adult, was not significant to me. I felt a clear conscience, but put in the bag the cheap metal ring I had worn in the hotel by the sea just in case. So I was ready for the next step. I kissed the boys goodnight and sank a third of a bottle of whisky and without saying goodnight to John went to bed.

The next day seemed a long day of agonizing over whether I was getting into something bizarre or foolish. The pain burned on and the routine continued and by six o'clock I was getting jumpy and nervous with an ever-increasing embarrassment tempting me to pick up the phone and call it all off. I sat with a glass of whisky trying to talk plans and facts to myself and I concluded that there could be several ends to the day. God might be real and I might be healed, or God was not real and all I had lost was a lot of pride and the last crumb of hope I had.

I picked up my naughty bag and held John's hand tightly as I said goodbye. I was glad that he was not going to be present to witness my humiliation. He was reluctant about it all but said he hoped it would work and that if I was not back by ten he would go to bed.

It was cold as I walked past the woods in the dark to Chris's house and I was glad that I could see a light on in his front window. He let me in with a welcoming smile and gently ushered me into his tiny front room. Horrors!! There were thousands of them there! I must run! However, because Chris was behind me there was no way out. I was in this like it or not! I tried to compose myself and be rational. I pulled myself together and counted the number of people present. Thousands were in fact six excluding myself! I started shaking with embarrassment and I felt as if there was a spotlight on me. This was a nightmare. Chris introduced me to the strangers and then gave me my instructions. I had to pray out loud that I was a sinner and confess my sins in front of them. WHAT!! I had to mean that I was truly sorry for going against God and determine not to do it again. I had to acknowledge that Jesus is the Son of God and the only way to God. I had to believe that he had lived 2000 years ago and been executed on a cross as the replacement punishment for my sin. I had to believe that he rose from the dead and is alive today. Then after all that, they would pray that he would come into my life and heal me.

If I could have run home I would have done. How did I get into this? I had never felt so embarrassed in all my life … give me a driving test any day! A blush like a red traffic light spread across my face and I became uncomfortably hot. Then things took a turn for the ridiculous. They explained that I was not to be alarmed if they started speaking in other languages. It was in the Bible that God gave his people a gift of praying in a language that they did not know! Well, this was going crazy. How could intelligent people get involved in something as mad as this ...? I looked around and assessed them, a chemist, a nurse, two graduates, and a dustman and his wife! Totally mad! I thought I could excuse the dust man. He had probably been led by the others, but not the rest. They were all barmy and I could not get out.

Derek spoke the prayers so that I in a shaky voice could repeat them. While we were praying the others were praying softly. I confessed that I was a sinner and gave my naughty bag to Derek. I said that I was truly sorry and in future would live God's way. I acknowledged that Jesus is the Son of God, that he died for my sin and is risen and alive today (although I did not believe that bit but I felt I was not being dishonest as I wanted to believe it). They then put their hands on me and asked the Holy Spirit to come and fill me and I caught other little bits of what they were praying. Derek was commanding the devil to loose his hold on me and claiming me for the kingdom of God and Chris and the others were babbling away in what sounded like rubbish. However, God had given me a sign that this was not rubbish but real because I happened to understand one word. Chris said loudly "bugaboo." How on earth would I know that word, you must be thinking?

My memory went back eighteen years to my schooldays when I was very happy. We had a temporary teacher for scripture and she came for just a term. I remembered being interested in things that she said because it was not all Bible. She had been a missionary for a tribe abroad and she told us about the Holy Spirit. I can remember her saying that she imagined him like a boiled sweet (why I shall never know!). She also talked about the devil and said the name the tribe gave him was "bugaboo," and I could remember a class of thirteen year olds falling apart laughing because it sounded so like a very familiar swear word! Here it was! Chris was addressing the devil on my behalf. This was real and beyond anything I had ever come across, far deeper than I could understand.

As they prayed, Jenny, the dustman's wife, put her hand on mine and I felt what I can best describe as an electric shock move up my right arm, across my back, and down my left arm. I was utterly bewildered and confused. The pain was still agony but something had definitely happened. I physically felt it. They all stopped praying and asked if the pain had gone. I told them something had happened but the pain was still there. They prayed for my protection and said that they would keep in touch and pray again if I wanted. As I left the house I was aware that I kept looking left and right as if crossing a road, trying to work out what had gone on.

The walk past the woods usually took ten minutes. It was my route back from school with the boys. Tonight I took it very slowly, trying to take it all in. As I walked, with each step I felt a bubbling joy rising up in me and I felt a love inside me that I had never felt before. The nearest adjective to describe it would be "passion." I was floating into ecstasy and as I crossed the road to my house, I knew without a doubt that Jesus is alive. It was beyond all my hopes and dreams. I had muddled through life seeing no purpose in it and with an indifference near to apathy. Now I felt motivated and enthusiastic and excited, feelings entirely foreign to me. I had expected either nothing would happen or I would be pain-free. I had never expected to return home still in excruciating pain but overjoyed and with a hope and a reason to live. There was another life to come, there is a heaven, and I knew that whatever I went through in this life I would live for eternity in this love and free from pain.

This was better and more than I had ever dreamt but I had not bargained for what was to come and what lay beyond the front door.

As I expected, John was in bed when I came in. He was not asleep as I thought he might be but lying in bed with the bedside light on.

"Has the pain gone?" he asked, preparing another way of comforting broken hopes and dreams

"No," I answered beaming from ear to ear, "but it doesn't matter anymore." I know for sure Jesus is alive and He will get me through. I could live for ever on the love I feel. I know he can do anything. He could even heal your blind eye (John had lost the sight in his left eye when he was seventeen).

John looked puzzled as I glowed. Then I realized that a miracle was taking place before my eyes. As I looked at John, I saw him as I had first seen him when we first met and I loved him SO much. He seemed to be glowing too and I realized how over the years my love for him had died. I thought our marriage was just stale and assumed that after twelve years that was what to expect. I had concluded that people who had been married for many years did so out of determination, commitment, and at times gritted teeth. Now I knew that was deception and God's intention for marriage was love for life. Jesus had given me back the love and respect for John that I had lost. He was healing our marriage. I knew now that he could see the far bigger picture. I thought I needed healing from pain. He knew I needed healing and restoration in my relationship with him and healing in my marriage which was so high on his list of priorities.

As we snuggled down in bed, a very perplexed John cuddled an ecstatic bundle of pain full of peace.

Chapter 6

Changed Forever

The next morning, two grinning boys leapt into bed with their sleeping mother unaware that they were to receive a reception unlike they had ever known. Instead of being resentfully sent back to bed, they were welcomed with smiles and cuddles. Their faces shone and I loved them so. Jesus's love for them was in me. I realized with shame that I had resented all the time they took from me and now I had all the time in the world for them. The realization of my selfishness brought me to tears. As they covered their faces with Weetabix I wiped it off with a patience I had never had and relished every moment of getting them ready for school. As we walked up the hill at their usual snail's pace, the endless chatter that usually drove me mad as I was still emerging from sleep at that time no longer irritated me and I really enjoyed their endless questions. At the school gate, I saw parents that I regularly saw and noticed a change here too. Mothers from the other side of the hill were noticeably poorer than we were and I had, to my shame, looked down on them and despised them. Now I was consumed with a passion for them and an overwhelming concern for their needs. They seemed to shine too. It was mind blowing.

On returning home, I made myself a cup of tea and decided to award myself ten minutes of reading the daily paper. Articles about violence and rape, which I usually read with indifference, actually sickened me. I felt physically sick. There was a whole new different me, reacting in a way totally foreign to me. The usual chores were a joy and I found that when I was preparing tea I could answer the boy's questions and stir a saucepan at the same time. I had concentration that I had not had. I had lost all the knots of anxiety in my stomach and felt totally relaxed.

In the evening, I put on a recording of the music for the film E.T. As a musician, I knew the thrill of the odd rare moment of musical perfection but as I listened, the music seemed to soar on to a higher unknown plane. It felt like worship and I can still never hear that music again without wanting to worship. It was sheer heaven. Out of habit, I went to pour myself a glass of whisky and, remembering how I hated what it did to me, put it back. It was not going to control my life any more. Jesus's love would get me through the pain.

When I lay down in bed, I thought I would just have a quick look at Robert's Bible. To my utter amazement, I found that I could understand it but not only that. It was speaking to me. I read, "I consider that our present sufferings are not worth comparing with the glory that will be revealed in us." (Romans 8: 18) and I knew it was true. We have approximately seventy years here of suffering and then something wonderful beyond our imaginings.

As I lay curled up beside John in bed, I considered the group's beliefs that a husband was in authority over his wife "Wives submit to your husbands" (1 Peter 3:1) I thought how opposite a view this was to that of modern society where

women have been so abused and undervalued and have had
to fight for their rights. I knew I had not been doing this and
had been belittling John and manipulating him to do what I
wanted and bossing him around. I observed the wives of the
group and found that their husbands were loving, strong,
and protective and yet giving them equal value and respect-
ing and considering their opinions and perspectives. They
were encouraged to find their strengths and achieve their
potentials. I could submit to men like this but the problem
was that this was not John. I knew I had the responsibility to
change my behaviour and trust that if I prayed, Jesus would
work in John's life to change him.

We live in a multicultural city and I found that as I took
the boys to the park, I was the only English person there
that day. Now I felt a love for the elderly Sikh men and their
grandchildren who were climbing the slide. This is the love
of God for them, now living in me.

John had observed all of this with curiosity. The woman
he had lived with so long had changed and he liked the
change. There was no more nagging and criticism. No
more arguing. Full whisky bottles were accumulating in the
cupboard and she no longer went to bed in a drunken stu-
por. A more or less non-existent physical relationship was
restored with a new passion. Whatever this was, he knew
this was real. This was not about going to church, living by
a list of dos and don'ts. This was about a person completely
changed by something that she claimed was Jesus and about
whom she knew little. She was associating with a group of
people who she respected and who had shown her respect
and who all had their own personal tale. She was trusting
Jesus to get her through.

This could be the end of the story but for us it was just
the beginning of twenty years of amazing events. It was a
journey that we might not have chosen to travel, through

the heights of ecstasy to the depths of despair. It has been twenty years of ever-increasing trust and certainty in Jesus, to whom I had been introduced.

It would be satisfying for all if I could end my story now with "they lived happily ever after!" but it was not to be that simple. Jesus had a plan that would take us to heights and depths that neither of us knew existed. I think it is very much for our benefit that we do not know the future because we would not have been prepared for it.

As I floated along in a stream of elation, I regularly kept in touch with the little group who were to become such supportive friends. They shared my delight and hope and taught me, answering all my questions with such patience, prayed with me, practically helped with the boys and gave of their time, even when it was not convenient. They befriended the bewildered John and shared all they had with us. I owe to them so much. I learnt such a lot in such a short time and it was difficult to keep my feet on the ground as I tried to make head or tail of the way my life had suddenly been turned upside down. Things that I had been brought up to believe were true were not, and things I understood to be lies were not necessarily so. I needed a lot of advice and instruction to learn this new way I had committed to take.

I found out that the little group not only shared all they had and their lives but they also met once a week to worship, pray, and listen to teaching tapes to increase their understanding. I thought that they knew everything but I soon found out that we were all learning alongside one another. Even Derek was learning and regularly was himself receiving instruction from his elder brother who was a leader in a Christian fellowship in the north. This was so different from what I had thought was "church" and I was so surprised to find out that there were little groups like this all over the country. My parents were a little alarmed in case I was getting involved in some sort of cult, but they let us get on with it having no other answer themselves to my problem. I think they were relieved that we had found help and support and the results seemed to be good.

I was learning a lot about God that I had never been told. The fact that he gives us freedom and not rules amazed me. That he wants a relationship with us tiny creatures and wants to communicate with us is what I wanted of a God. I soon realized that all my life he had been giving me choices and as I made them had been setting out the next steps for me. I had often made wrong choices for which I suffered the consequences, but he had always given me a way through and had been working for my good. He gave me the freedom of choice to marry John and as he saw things were going wrong was waiting for me to ask for help so that he could intervene. How independent we human beings are that we will allow our choices to lead us into such depths that we are forced to cry "help!" or die. I had often puzzled about the seeming contradiction that a God who claimed to be perfect love could send people to Hell. Now I understood that he does not. We send ourselves there by our choices.

In just one week, so many billions of thoughts rushed through my mind. I looked back over my life and could see concrete evidence of God's protection for me, even as a small child. One particular event really stood out in my memory. I attended a school that had a new building next to it. We called it the skyscraper because it was about twenty storeys high! Little did we small children know how high skyscrapers were to become in our lifetime. The skyscraper consisted of offices which overlooked the school on one side and the bus stops on the other. One day after school, I was waiting on my own for my bus home. I was about ten at the time, when a man came and stood uncomfortably near to me. He asked "parlez-vous Francais?" which I understood because I had just been taught French that year. I had been regularly instructed by my parents and teachers not to speak to strangers, but I had also been taught not to be impolite. This gave me an uncomfortable dilemma, and so I replied "Oui" and turned my back on him to end the conversation. He turned to the front of me and persisted to want to talk and I became increasingly unhappy.

"Please make the bus come soon," I thought. Is a thought in a child's mind a prayer? The bus still did not come and as I was starting to panic he said, "Would you like to come for a walk with me?" As I replied, "No," a lady appeared as if from nowhere, much to my relief, and he went away very quickly. She asked if I was alright and had he hurt me. I relayed to her all that was said and added that I was frightened. She explained that she worked in the skyscraper and had been watching as she typed and had been increasingly concerned. She waited until I was on the bus before returning to work. What would have happened to me if she had not been there and had the presence of mind to come down? I hate to think, but I saw this as one of hundreds of examples that I could now see were God protecting me all through my life.

So, returning to the present, I now had to make new choices and a difficult one was around the corner. As time went on the everyday pressures of life ate away at my peace and the constant pain pulled me down from my joy. Yes, I no longer turned to the whisky but at times it was so tempting. How could I handle the pain? All the group were agreed that Jesus does not start something without finishing it and they all agreed that he did not want me in pain and so we decided to keep praying regularly to see what would happen. Now was my dilemma because I still had an appointment arranged with the hypnotherapist. Having repented of my involvement in this and particularly with the feeling of threat, I had no desire to go. I understood a little of what had made me so uncomfortable as I had been taught just a little about the spiritual war going on that we cannot see and I most definitely did not want demons attacking me. I was in enough trouble as it was! We all agreed, I should cancel the appointment but then I hit an unexpected problem. John, not understanding at the time what this was all about, wanted me to go and was against their decision. Despite my pleading, he insisted that I went just once more. What a choice! On one hand I was being taught to submit to my husband and on the other was advised not to do something that he wanted. What should I do? To this day, I am not sure I made the right choice, but I decided to please John and go, trusting that God would protect me from the threats. We decided that I should just go and say thank you and take an offering of a bottle of brandy and say goodbye.

It was not a comfortable Pamela in the taxi clutching the bottle. I made my way up the drive of laurel bushes with an increasing apprehension and knocking knees. As I was welcomed in, I held out the bottle in front of me as if to guard me and weakly spluttered

"I've just come to say thank you and goodbye. I'm better now so I don't need to come anymore. Thank you for your time and care."

The bottle of brandy was gratefully received but it was not going to be that easy. I was not going to be let off that lightly. "Thank you," the tall figure responded and then added something that I had not expected. "I promised your Father that I would take care of you and I can't leave you like this. I want you to come into my consulting room and convince me that you are better and then we will say goodbye."

Oh! What a nightmare! What had I let myself in for! Praying silently for Jesus to protect me, I followed him into the dimly lit den of demons. I could feel the threat again and it was as if unseen beings were menacing me. I obediently sat down as requested on the dreaded black leather couch and shook as it reclined backwards. "Imagine yourself in your favourite place," I was instructed. I thought of Herm and remembered how beautiful it was. "I will now start counting down and as I do relax and I will ask you questions to see if you are better," he explained. Alarm bells rang in my head. I just could not do this but what else could I do? I prayed for my protection but had no idea, having been a Christian for such a little time, what to do. All I knew was The Lord's Prayer, so I decided that as he counted I would say it silently to myself so as to block out his words. As I started "Our Father" ..., I felt a tingling feeling and a bit of a glow. As soon as he had stopped, he asked me a question and I decided that everything he asked I would reply by relating to Jesus or avoiding the question. I cannot remember all the questions that came at me interrupted by counting and silent prayers, but I remember one. He asked me to imagine a kettle and asked what colour it was. I replied that it was red. He then proceeded to question me as to why it was red and my response was that he had asked me to give it a colour and red seemed as valid as any other colour, but it could be blue, silver, or yellow if he wanted. He then asked me to say when it was boiling. I replied that it would never boil, and when he puzzled, enquired why, I frustrated him by saying that it was a type of kettle that never boiled! After more counting and questions, he asked me to imagine a blackboard and draw something on it. Having decided to relate everything I could to Jesus, I drew a cross. He asked what colour cross it was. When I replied brown he asked why and I continued because it is made of wood. "Why is it made of wood?" he persisted.

"Because it is Jesus's cross," was my answer.

"Now put your pain on the blackboard and tell me where it is," he instructed.

"It's in the centre of the cross," I concluded.

"Sit up," he requested kindly. "I cannot help you," was his conclusion. "I teach people to go through all the stages you have gone through and when they get to the blackboard I teach them to imagine a box and then put their pain or problems in it and give it away. You have given your pain to Jesus and I can do nothing for you. You are better. Now, please tell me what has happened since I last saw you." I respectfully recited the amazing events that had occurred and he concluded, "I am pleased for you. If someone would prove it to me, I would believe it." He had missed what so many miss, that it will never be proved to us because it is all about faith which would be non-existent with proof. I hope God was giving him a chance to take some step of faith that would set him on the way as I'm sure he cared about hurting people and, as we all do, needed Jesus for himself as well as to help others. We said an amicable goodbye, him holding his bottle of brandy and me returning "better" and in excruciating pain.

Chapter 7

Charlie Attacked

Safe and relieved and mildly pleased with the outcome of it all, I returned to report to the group and we thanked God for his protection. We then settled down to address the next problem. "Why was I still in pain when they had prayed for healing?" There was no doubt that God had given me a miracle and we all accepted that he knew what he was doing, but we wanted some clues so that we could work with him. We were all overwhelmed with what had happened but were all relatively new to all of this. Regularly, Derek would phone his brother for advice and we kept meeting to pray but I was not getting any better.

Two reasons why came to our minds. The first was that, although curious and supportive, John was not actively involved and we needed him. I especially recognized that there were changes that only God could bring about in his life and they would improve my life tremendously. We started to pray for him and one of us had a vision of John with a knife in his heart, which Jesus gently pulled out. They asked me if I knew what it could be and the only thing I could think of was losing his sight, so we prayed that God would give him back his sight. We believed for a miracle. The other thing they picked up was that I was very negative. That was all I had ever known. God requires faith and I had taken, even if pushed, a step of faith in getting involved in the first place. Now, they felt God was requiring me to exercise faith for my healing and wanted me to be more positive. Miracles are instant, but healing takes time. I think even now some of the churches get confused over this. I was advised to daily keep thanking God for my healing and to positively claim it, which I did.

I had no problem thanking God daily, but to say the pain had gone, in faith, seemed ridiculous to me but I accepted that they were all more intelligent than I was and when I had done as they suggested before, the results were good so I would do it. Every time someone asked how I was, I replied that I was healed, which pleased everyone except me!

Every week John lent me the car and I did our weekly shopping as there was quite a lot with two hungry mouths constantly needing feeding. It was not my favourite job. Pushing a loaded trolley round a crowded supermarket was tiring and the background music that was played made it very difficult for me to think with the pain. Today, however, there was to be a pleasant surprise for me. There by the vegetables was Terry the dustman. He greeted me with a warm smile that made me feel as if I was part of something special and very privileged. It was like being part of an elite secret club, and his smile said "you belong."

"Hello Pam," he beamed, "How's things?"

"OK," I replied with faith!

"How is the pain?" he continued with genuine concern.

"It's gone," was my faithful answer, but then I added quietly and hesitantly. "The only problem now, Terry, is that I can still feel it."

"Well I don't believe it has gone," he announced, stunning me. Why was he disagreeing with all the rest with all their experience and qualifications? I was confused.

"Why? Explain to me," I questioned in a quiet squeaky voice.

"I don't believe it's gone. It 'aint gone' cause it's still here." How ridiculously simple and true. It took a dustman to see sense! In two minutes, he had lifted a burden of confusion off me and then proceeded to bring in words of hope. This taught me a lot. How easily people with great need could be brainwashed by cults no matter how intelligent and how much we need to listen to all people without judging them. We all have something of value to offer one another. I am so grateful to God that he took me in my vulnerability to his people who, although inexperienced, were following truth and adaptable and teachable and who had hearts of love for Jesus and their fellow beings. Our lives have all moved on in different directions now but twenty years on I still contact them and value their prayers, advice and friendship. You are a special bunch!

As my pain in my face and my pelvis started to attack my knees and make walking difficult, John and I faced what we thought was our next hurdle and it could be summed up in one word, "Charlie." I have told you how I could identify God's protection in my life and it was the same for Charlie. Not only did he have his breakfast experience but God also placed just the right people in his life at the right time to help him. When he was a tiny baby, my brother Jim was training to be an optician. He wanted to examine a baby's eyes and Charlie was volunteered. When Jim said "Your baby can't see," I politely told him to return to college and learn. He regularly checked Charlie's eyes and as soon as he left college and began his employment as an ophthalmic optician, Charlie was one of his first patients. Charlie was well known in the neighbourhood for his placid beaming smile and for being the only baby in a pushchair wearing little round spectacles. For "best" he had a little gold pair that Jim gave him and he looked cute! We have been told since by other local opticians that if Charlie's problem had not been treated before the age of one, he would never have seen properly, even with spectacles. I am so grateful.

Charlie also had some narrow squeaks! Almost as if something was attacking his life even from within the womb. We now recognize the enemy as Satan but at the time just felt everything was against us. John was known for having fads, and one year when Charlie was two, the fad was wine making. The kitchen was taken over with demi-johns, bottles, and corks, and it was an extremely hot summer. One day, John was concerned that the heat would interfere with the fermenting process and instructed me to put the demi-johns on the bedroom floor, out of the direct sunlight. Charlie found this quite interesting and followed me around transporting bottles up the stairs.

Twenty years ago, the air locks used for wine making were made of glass and Charlie was fascinated by watching the bubbles moving around in the air lock. He, unlike Sam, was a very placid obedient and predictable child and when he asked if he could watch the bubbles I said "Yes, but don't touch," knowing full well that he could be trusted. I left him crouched down saying "blup, blup," happily and went into the next room to change Sam's nappy. When I heard the scream I moved fast! Charlie rarely cried yet alone screamed. On rushing into the bedroom, a murder scene met my eyes! The white wardrobe was covered in blood, there was blood all over the carpet and the window ledge and I could not see Charlie's face for blood. I picked up Charlie and ran with him into Sam's room, grabbed a clean nappy and sat him in the bath, telling him to press it tight against his face which with his usual obedience he did. I then did something instinctive. Normally, a level-headed person in such a situation would have dialled 999 but I rang my mother and shouted "GET HERE!" Thankfully, she picked up the urgency of the situation and asked my father not to leave for surgery until she got back. I carried the half-dressed Sam under one arm and the bleeding Charlie clutching his nappy against his head and we leapt into the car leaving all the doors open. Grandpa was waiting only a few minutes away and as soon as he saw Charlie he took him up to his study, laid him on the couch, and proceeded to stitch up his head. He had no anaesthetic and to inflict pain on the little person he loved so much hurt him more than Charlie. As Charlie was cleaned up, an ice cream van stopped in the road and Charlie was rewarded with an ice cream and we were all rewarded with large whiskies. We were all shaking. It turned out that Charlie crouching down had leant over his centre of gravity and toppled onto the glass air lock which had broken and severed his temporal artery. His life had been saved and God's faithful protection of us proved yet again. It was only as we recovered that I remembered to phone a shocked John to explain that the blood all up the stairs was not a sign that I had "lost it" and killed the constantly screaming Sam but that we were alright, much to his relief.

So, now it was Charlie's turn for yet another attack. As I had mentioned, I had problems during my pregnancy but because Charlie was so contented and happy I did not notice anything wrong for some time. When Sam was old enough to sit up, it was much easier to put them in the bath together and it was much more fun for them. It was only seeing them side by side one day that I noticed that Charlie and Sam's backs were very different. Sam's was very smooth and straight and yet Charlie's had a large lump in it.

I asked Grandpa to take a look sometime and he agreed that all was not well and arranged for an orthopaedic consultant to examine him. We were told Charlie had a seriously bent spine and that he would need extensive surgery to correct this when he was about eight. There were serious risks attached to the surgery but if we chose to leave it, Charlie in his teens would have keeled over, compressing his lungs and becoming severely deformed. We were agreed that the risks of the operation were the lesser evil but were extremely concerned about it and tended to push it to the back of our minds.

Now, Charlie was seven and we were having to start to face this with him. I always reckon God knew what Charlie would have to face physically in his life and had given him such a contented placid and steady personality in order to cope. I told the group about Charlie's problem and we started praying for God to heal him. Not one of us had any doubt that Jesus through the work of the Holy Spirit could perform a miracle for Charlie, but we recognized that God sometimes uses doctors to heal. We did not want Charlie to suffer or to give him a hope of a miracle without being 100% sure that that was what God wanted to do. Derek decided to enlist the help and prayers of his brother and the fellowship they belonged to for support for us. John had observed the events and changes of the previous few months with curiosity and because he was treated with respect and friendship with no strings attached always welcomed Derek and Chris if they called.

One evening, they arrived unexpectedly with four cans of beer and a proposition. They asked John how he felt about the forthcoming surgery for Charlie and said that they believed God wanted the best for Charlie and offered, if John wanted, to take us and the boys up north to the fellowship and arrange a night of prayers for Charlie. John's response was to appreciate their concern and respect for him but to say, "I don't believe it but if there is a God I think Charlie should not be denied a chance so I will take him if you will sort it out."

I was really excited. I really believed that Charlie would be miraculously healed, that John would be instantly changed and perfect, and that we all would live happily ever after! I did not want Charlie to suffer and could not believe a loving God would deny a little boy his healing, especially as he had had breakfast with him!

Still being an unrepentant snob, I took Charlie down to the local shops and had his feet measured for some new shoes. I could not have him going to meet such amazingly godly people in his tatty old ones! I packed with hyperactive enthusiasm but was very careful not to give Charlie any expectations of the weekend. All he knew was that his back was bent and we were going to ask Jesus if he would make it better. We bundled into the car with Sam making his usual squeally protests and arrived at the appointed venue at the university. Unlike traditional churches, this church or fellowship, as it was called, had their main meeting on a Friday night. The members of the fellowship knew about us from Derek's phone calls and were extremely welcoming and hospitable and we were granted the overwhelming privilege of meeting their leader who appeared to me, as a new Christian, to be almost God himself! He was a tall, quietly spoken man with great dignity and the fact that he was trusted by God to be getting involved in God's work in China made him seem so way above me as I did not even yet know where half the books in the Bible were!

I shall always remember the Friday night when they prayed for Charlie. So many emotions were going round in my head. I desperately wanted Charlie to be spared the suffering of surgery. I was concerned at what John would make of the gathering. I had only been to Chris's house but I knew some of the worship and prayer. If John was expecting a service like the Anglican one we had for our wedding, I knew he was in for a shock. We gathered in an octagonal room with banked chairs and a group of musicians at the front with guitars and keyboards. I must admit that as a professional musician, I found the modern worship extremely dissatisfying and unmusical. It was repetitively uninteresting and was one of the aspects of my entrance into the church that I found most difficult.

I never liked being the centre of attention and so when we were asked to go out to the front with Charlie, I felt so exposed and I wondered exactly what John felt. If this was difficult for me, how was it for him?

A small chair was placed for Charlie and the tall composed leader, Colin, bent gently down to Charlie's level. "Do you believe Jesus could make you better?" he asked quietly and calmly.

"Oh Yes," replied Charlie without a hesitation.

"Right we'll ask him," Colin said and everyone at the front linked hands with John and me as Colin placed his hands on Charlie and prayed for him. The meeting then continued for a while and we returned to the home where we were staying. As we put Charlie to bed I was devastated as we took off his shirt and there was the lump on his back just as before. John could not understand how I felt as he had gone expecting nothing and nothing was what we had got. "Don't be disappointed," he comforted. "Just look on this as a nice weekend away."

However, I was so very disappointed, but the one good thing about the whole evening was that Charlie was completely content and John had found the meeting an interesting experience.

During the weekend, we learnt a lot about how the fellowship lived. It was not a community in that they lost their individuality and identity, but they all lived close to one another, as we lived close to Chris, and they shared all aspects of their life, their food, their property, their problems, and their joys. Their lives intermingled giving a strength and a security that was missing in our lives, although there to an extent.

It was sunny on the Sunday we were due to return home and they had planned a picnic in the park for the children to enjoy, which we were invited to share. While we were enjoying ourselves, Colin and one of the other leaders came over to John and announced that they had been praying as to why Charlie had not been healed because it was their experience that Jesus never does nothing. It was their understanding that Jesus had said there was something wrong with Charlie's legs. We were puzzled because the problem was in his back but not his legs. They asked John's permission to examine Charlie saying confidently "If God says it's his legs then it's his legs." They lay a comfortable Charlie down under a large oak tree and held his legs out together. "Look!" they exclaimed and we could all see that he had one leg considerably shorter than the other. They agreed to pray about this and stood me at Charlie's head and John at his feet whilst all the crowd gathered around to see what would happen. As people started praising Jesus and Colin prayed, I watched intently and gasped as Charlie's left leg started to move. I thought "I am his mother and I don't want him to go into hospital and I am imagining this," and so I looked up to see what everyone else was doing. Everyone was celebrating. An adamant Charlie sat up and said "That was a cheating! Someone pulled my foot!" But no one had even touched him! I knew where I would get the truth with no hype. I walked round to John and said "Nothing happened, did it?"

"I don't understand it," was his reply, "but I saw it. His leg grew!"

We mused over this all the way home. Now, we had Charlie with two legs the same length but still a very deformed back. What on earth was going on?

Charlie whined all the way home which was extremely out of character for him and continued to whine and complain all the next day that his feet were hurting. Sam's constant screaming always drove me to distraction, but Charlie's whining was more than my patience could stand. I examined his feet and could find nothing wrong but because this was Charlie, I took his complaining seriously and as we were passing decided to take him back to the shoe shop. The same assistant who had sold the proud Charlie his new shoes re-measured him with the same gauge and we were mystified as to the fact that his feet were one size larger! She was adamant that her first measurement was correct but fitted with larger shoes, a peaceful Charlie returned to his everyday life.

That evening, John and I mused over the events of the weekend and agreed that we were puzzled but would obviously have to continue down the road to spinal surgery for Charlie and began to prepare him for this. I hoped that in the following months God might cause the deformity to correct. Time would tell, meanwhile our daily lives had to continue. We had, thankfully, no idea how traumatic and difficult these months were to be.

Chapter 8

⌒

Meaning Business

The little prayer group and I were quite excited because three days after our weekend away, Billy Graham was due to visit our city, and we had been praying for many of our friends to go to hear what he had to say. My greatest hope was that John would go, but it was unlikely. The evening before the event, I gently asked if he would like to come with me and to my amazement he was quite enthusiastic about this. I was delighted because I knew that if he found Jesus as I had, life for our family would be so much better and I wanted us to share this.

On reflection, I think that the fact that the campaign was to be in the grounds of John's favourite football team was an added incentive!

I felt nervous as I made my way through that Wednesday and was very uneasy as we joined a coach load of bouncy enthusiastic Christians dragging alongside them bemused and bewildered friends. "This will be a real turn off for John," I thought and increasingly wished we had stayed at home. Once we entered the football ground, I felt a little better as this was familiar for John but my discomfort increased as we began to sing hymns and the Christians became more and more enthusiastic. I knew that John would not be influenced by the emotions of others and would most likely back off.

We listened as Billy Graham gave his message about Jesus and then received the collection plate. We placed our little offering on top of that of a young student next to us, and later I heard from John that this young man's gift to God of an amount that he obviously could not afford said as much as the message itself!

At the end of the evening, Billy Graham asked anyone who wanted to commit their lives to Jesus to go onto the football pitch, and to my amazement, John turned to me and said, "I just have to go." I sat and watched him make his way through the crowds and saw his tiny figure amongst the masses meet up with another person. I knew John well enough to know that this commitment was not a light decision influenced by others, but a long thought out and serious intention.

This would change our lives for ever, but little did I know how much harder our lives were to become. I thought everything would be so much easier with us sharing the same belief and I could only gain. There is a cost to following Jesus that John had considered very seriously. A lot of people give the impression that once you are a Christian, life becomes a bed of roses. This is, I have found, not truth. To take up your cross and follow is so painful at times as we were to find out.

When John returned to his seat, he was carrying a piece of paper. He had had to tick a relevant box, choosing between (1) I am a Christian, (2) I am a Christian and have slipped backwards, (3) I am not a Christian and want to know more, and (4) I want to commit my life to Jesus. The choice for John had been confusing and he said that he was not sure which box to tick. When he ticked box (1), he then thought "When did I become A Christian?" and realized that it had been on the night that Charlie was prayed for that he had made a decision in his heart to follow Jesus.

On returning home, we sat and prayed together for the first time, and my world was full of hope for healing for me and Charlie now that John was with us. Christianity is about a battle between good and evil, and with John fighting for his family, there was hope. I had no idea how fierce the fighting would be.

I think many people attend church without fully understanding Jesus's requirement for repentance. I thought it meant saying sorry to God and myself had not fully grasped that it also meant doing an about turn and changing old ways to God's ways. We were quickly with the teaching and help of others to learn about this, and both of us being serious about our commitment set about putting it into practice. I knew John meant business and it was soon evident as he made his way down the garden carrying a pile of brown envelopes in the dusky light. At work, the men in the office subscribed to "men's magazines" that were passed around in brown envelopes, which always ended up at our house. John had encouraged me to read them thinking it might add excitement to our married life. I hated them and, concerned that the boys might see them, insisted that if John had to keep them they should stay up in the loft away from Charlie and Sam. Now watching him set fire to them on the bonfire heap, I knew just how serious about this he was, and as it was only making things happier for me, I did not feel the pain of cost. John instantly stopped swearing and I was so grateful for this having always been unhappy about the example it set for the boys. At last, we were going in the same direction and along the same path. Everyone noticed the change in John, especially his colleagues at work. He was told that he had lost his sense of humour, but in fact, it was not lost but changed. Dirty jokes were no longer funny. A "no swearing John" was observed with curiosity. One of the secretaries came up to John one day at coffee time and said "I have heard that you have become a Christian"

"How do you know?" puzzled John who had been keeping it all very quiet and private.

"I heard it in the ladies loo!" was the amusing reply. "It's amazing what we ladies talk about in the loo!" That is obviously where we should go if we want to know anything!

John took a lot of "stick" at work and found the support of the group vital in the early days. However, he knew that he could not always rely on these men as most had plans to move up North to the Christian fellowship because they believed that this was what God was asking them to do and they would not be here for ever. As we watched the "For Sale" signs go up one by one on their houses, we had to ask the question, "should we go too?" It meant changes of job, leaving family, changes of school, things we had never thought would be issues for us. The firm ground under our feet suddenly became very wobbly.

Each member of the group had their own problems and we continued to meet regularly to support each other and we also went to the fellowship as often as we could. For John and me, the problem was still my severe pain and Charlie's forthcoming surgery. I was desperately asking Jesus why He had not healed me and it was at this time that I had a most unusual dream. It was very short and so vivid that it stood out as unusual enough to make me think. I dreamed that I was crossing our road wearing a beautiful wedding dress and that I walked into the woods opposite our house. There, sitting on a bench, was my father's partner, my doctor, and I walked up to him and handed him an invitation to my wedding. When I woke I thought it was a really odd thing to have dreamt. It was only months later that I could look back and see that God was trying to prepare me for what he was about to do and to reassure me in the trauma to come that he was in control and working for my good. If only I had recognized this, it might not have been so difficult but it is easy to look back with wisdom.

It was a completely new thing for me to find that the Bible spoke to me and now I could see its relevance. As I continued to ask "why," I searched it for clues. It is years ago now and I cannot find the verse that gave me some of my answer, but I clearly remember that the ending said "still you keep on sinning."

This puzzled me as I had given up anything that I knew was wrong and now so too had John. I asked Jesus to show me what it was that I was doing that prevented my healing and the answer came in a most unexpected way (as usually seems to happen with God).

It was my regular weekly job to go down to the local supermarket to buy our food for the week. As a friend had a birthday coming, I went into the stationers to buy a card after I had loaded the heavy shopping into the car. As I was choosing the card, I noticed my father's practice nurse nearby. I had not seen her for at least a couple of years even though she lived in my road. I knew that she was a committed Christian who was involved in missionary work and I knew that she had been teased unmercifully in the surgery. I now realized that it must often have been very difficult for her but she always handled it with a gentle sense of humour. She spotted me choosing my card and came over to ask how I was. I knew she would be thrilled that we had found Jesus and the glow on her face as I told her our story said it all. She listened intently as I explained my confusion over this unknown sin and then she gently said, "I think you should come back for a cup of tea." I drove to her house and happily left all our frozen food thawing out in the boot of the car as I followed her into her front room. This was so important to me. Did she have an answer for me?

We enjoyed a drink together and then she suggested that we pray. I watched a shimmering glow spread across her face as she started to talk to the Jesus she loved so much. I have never since seen anyone glow like that. "Have you repented of the Freemasonry?" she asked. I did not under-stand. My father was a freemason and all that it meant to me was glamorous ladies' evenings full of beautiful dresses and delicious food. I loved them. What could be wrong with that? Also surely raising money for charity was a good thing. My father, who loved and cared for so many people, would not be involved in something that did harm and even if he was, I was not a freemason. She patiently explained that freemasonry and Christianity were incompatible and that I needed to repent of any involvement, especially saying the graces to their God at the ladies' nights. She prayed for me and my father and then we parted, and it was years before I met her again.

After I had carried the soggy remains of our frozen food into the house, I phoned Derek, who was often available in the day, and told him what had happened. He confirmed that this was something we needed to pray about and arranged to phone the fellowship for more information. As before, he asked me to bring anything masonic in the house to the group before we prayed. This made me very sad. I had a masonic brooch given to me by my much loved Grandpa when I was a child. I treasured it and did not want to let it go. However, the choice was brooch or pain and it had to go. John came with me to the group and we threw it in the bin and prayed to repent of any involvement. The words from the fellowship were stronger than the gentle nurse's explanation. They actually declared freemasonry to be occult and gave scriptural evidence for us. We knew this meant no more lovely ladies' nights, no more masonic coach trips, and ahead loomed the dilemma of how to explain our rejection of this in an acceptable way. We were advised to say as little as possible and I was to leave it to John. That though gave me no peace.

I could not sleep that night. It did not tie up. The majority of patients in our town loved my father. He was held in high esteem. He had cared for others often at his own cost and was so gentle and reassuring. He would never do anything bad. If what I had found out was true, I was sure he was ignorant of the dark side of this. He never went to church, having no time for what he saw as hypocrisy, and my mother had said freemasonry was his church. If it was occult, then according to the Bible, the person I loved so much was in ignorance and going to hell. I lay in bed panicking and saying "Jesus, what do I do?" John was snoring contentedly beside me and I did not want to wake him to share my concern. I decided to put into practice the relaxation exercises that I had done at ante natal classes and eventually dropped off to sleep. It was then that I had another of these vivid unusual dreams. I dreamt that I was standing in front of what I can only describe as a large refrigerator of the brightest light. Out of this light came a voice whose words were so specific. They were "Do not say a word to your father as I have set aside for him a man at Brewick police station." I woke with a start, the words ringing clearly in my head, never to be forgotten. Was I mad? I wondered.

When I told John he just swept it aside with a "Forget it, don't worry" and set off for work.

Half way through sorting a pile of small socks into pairs, the phone rang. It was my mother who usually phoned each day. We chatted about the boys and her cleaner's

latest news and then she said "I'll have to go, we are going
out to lunch." This was not unusual as they often went out
to lunch and so I did not take much interest, but to be polite
asked, "Where are you going?"

"I'm not sure," she replied. "We are taking out the new
post mortem room attendant from Brewick police station.
I've not yet met him."

Her words were as clear as those of the dream and so I
planned to follow it up. Two days later, I asked her casually
if they had had a nice lunch. "Oh yes," was her reply. "Fred
was such a nice man, you would have liked him. He is a
Christian and a counsellor for Billy Graham's work."

I was staggered. This was more than a coincidence. God
was in control of an enormous plan that we were caught
up in. It was exciting and scary but I did have peace that
my father would be alright. I met Fred and found him to
be a man of about the same age as my father and as they
worked together, I watched respect grow into friendship.
I never told Fred about the dream because if it was God
at work, I did not want to engineer anything or put any
pressure on him. I did voice my concerns with him and he
agreed that freemasonry was occult but wisely reassured
me saying "Let's wait for God's time. We don't want to
get up people's noses." How much I still have to learn of
that sensitivity to God and gentleness towards people. I
would have gone in all guns firing and made a complete
mess of it. I look back and cringe at the mistakes I have
made. God is working his purpose out and how often do
we think we have to do it for him and try to do it our way.
It is so good to know that he takes our worst mistakes and
makes them into successes for the glory of his son Jesus. I
reckon that is why He always seems to be most powerful
when we have just about given up so that only Jesus can
have the glory.

The leaves on the oak trees in the woods were beginning to turn golden and I could see my favourite time of year approaching. I loved to take Charlie and Sam to collect conkers and wander amongst the crunchy leaves, although I hated the inevitable cleaning dog dirt off the shoes afterwards! Past the school and down the hill, the "For Sale" sign on Derek's house now read "Sold" and we felt vulnerable as he left. He had always been the source of steady encouragement and always was available to help. We had hung onto him. Chris had handed in his notice and his house was for sale too and so we considered our future. It seemed plain to me that we should also go. Why would God involve us in something so unique and then take it away? In my heart, I was prepared to go. In fact, the boys were supposed to have new blue sweaters for the coming term at school, but I was so sure they would not be staying there that I bought grey ones thinking they would not stand out as wrong and could be used in their next schools. When we visited the fellowship, John discussed our moving with the elders and recognizing that we were new Christians, they quizzed John as to what God had said about our future. We were going purely on feelings and so they wisely said that they were unhappy for us to move with a family unless John had a job to go to. Thus began the unsettling job search. John was experienced and well qualified and jobs that seemed tailor-made for him were available but with each application there was rejection. We could not go. Nor too could Chris who could not sell his house. We said goodbye to my precious dustman as his wife reluctantly left the new kitchen she had waited a few years for and moved with their children into borrowed accommodation belonging to a family in the fellowship. We were frustrated at the hold ups and the wait and I had a feeling that I would never be healed as long as we stayed where we were. We had only Chris now and our situation was pretty desperate. It seemed to miss my thinking that we had Jesus who had a different and better plan than ours that encompassed a far greater picture.

As we waited, I realized that something in me of great significance had changed. Since I repented of freemasonry, I realized that I was always doing what my father wanted and not what John wanted. John was not the head of his family, my father was. If there was a difference in any situation between their opinions, I would always do as my father wanted. His motives in all of this were to see his daughter and his grandchildren have what he thought was the best for them. There was a dark side to this that in so doing he was undermining John's authority and making him feel that he had no say in our lives. I could see how I had never grown up and left home and how I manipulated John into doing what my father wanted. This had to change and I found out for the first time the cost of following Jesus. I had to choose between my father and my husband and our marriage. It was so hard. My parents had noticed major changes in us and were perplexed and now I knew that the stand I was being asked to take would make them feel rejected and hurt. Our too close relationship was never to be the same again.

Chapter 9

The Knife

It began with the famous battle of the hall carpet. The carpet had been a gift from my father to me on my 21st birthday and due to Sam's amazing technique of sitting on the top stair, lifting his little legs, and sliding at high speed to the bottom was becoming very threadbare. My father wanted us to buy a new one, wanting the best for us, but John did not want to buy one until he could afford it. I was put under enormous pressure to manipulate John into submission but I, for the first time, stood with John and agreed with him. It was really hard. My father even offered to buy the carpet, but his offer was turned down. For the good of our marriage, we had to unite and win this and to let my father know in kind but firm ways that what John decided was to happen for his family was what would happen. We won, but it hurt me so much to see the father I loved so much bewildered and hurt. It was a major change that had to happen and without my realization of this, I could never have been free to go with John where God wanted us to go. I would have stayed tied to my parents. This was something that I had to work through before God could move us and was a major healing in our marriage. I asked Jesus to take away my pain, but he knew that my marriage needed healing first for our sakes and those of the boys. I thought our marriage was stale, but Jesus knew it was in a far worse state than I realized. He was beginning to bring about the reality of my wedding dress dream, but at the time I did not recognize this and I had no idea the battle and heartache we were to go into.

John was not a man to waste time and so whilst he was searching for a job to move us up north, he set about intensely seeking God as to why I was not healed. He met regularly with Chris and we often spent weekends at the fellowship. We knew we needed teaching and we knew we were in a desperate state. Alone with Chris, all week we listened to teaching tapes and brought ourselves a little book called "Every day with Jesus "by Selwyn Hughes. It contained a few short Bible verses for each day and gave an explanation of them and showed us how to apply it. It was very helpful for someone unwell because it was not too long or complicated and it never failed to amaze me that in that time of isolation nearly every page was so relevant to what I was to face each day.

Just as I had gathered my "naughty bag," John started a serious clean up of his life and our house. When I look back, I think we became perhaps too extreme but we were really serious about our commitment to God and wanted nothing between him and us. Out went books, magazines, our Chinese bowls with five toed dragons on, John's beloved books of Escher drawings, which now gave him the shivers..... we could have had a car boot sale if they had been around in those days! Also out went any unclean animals including, to Sam's horror, Kermit the frog (for the comfort of the reader and Sam soon to be replaced by Easter Chicken and Scotty bear). We tried to show God we would do anything he asked, and if we got it wrong, he knew our hearts. We studied books and tapes on blocks to healing and searched ourselves for unforgiveness and unbelief. We did everything we could but beg as we may I was still in agony. John seemed to spend more and more time praying silently by himself and seemed to become unnervingly quieter for such an extrovert. One evening he took a big sigh and said "I think I'll go to Scotland and see Robert."

"Great!" was my reaction, "I'll pack and come too." The thought of that reassuring gentle Scottish voice was so appealing. I was puzzled at John's reaction to my enthusiasm. I thought he would be pleased, but he quietly told me he wanted to go alone. "Why?" Since we had become Christians this was the first time he was excluding me from part of his life. I started to worry. Were we going back into the old ways of him leading a separate life from me? It was early days in our new life and trust and security were extremely shaky. I agreed to him going and I knew Robert could only do me good. I trusted that man's opinions and authority, but I was disappointed to have to stay at home looking after the boys on my own again. It had been such a support in my pain that John had been taking his responsibilities as a father and helping me, and now, I had to go it alone again.

I comforted myself with the thought that it would be a few weeks before the busy Robert could see John, and in the meantime, I could look forward to a visit from my beloved brother and his wife and new baby. They had never stayed with us before and I wanted to give them a lovely time. I started planning the moving around of beds and looking for meals that were easy to cook if the pain was so bad I could not think, and I planned a visit to a living museum to interest them. I bought chocolates for treats and beer for Jim and flowers for Louise, and Chris lent us his travel cot for the baby. It was going to be a happy and exciting time.

I did not just plan it; I involved God in it, praying everyday for ideas of how I could make it a real treat for them. They were due to arrive on Friday for the weekend and so I spent a little extra time praying on Thursday morning in preparation for the time ahead. As usual, I read my Every Day With Jesus to see if there would be some guidance for me. It was so often so applicable. However, the reading for that day seemed out of the flow of the previous days. It was the story of a woman caught in adultery being brought to Jesus before her due punishment of being stoned and how Jesus put a stop to her death, called her to repentance, and forgave her. I sat in my chair and puzzled. Surely Jim would not have..... no, he never would......we were brought up with strict morals.....adultery was not on. But, no doubt there was temptation but I thought I knew Jim enough to be sure that he was strong enough to resist that. I was sure he loved Louise and the baby. He lived a distance away and had done so since leaving university and although we phoned often we rarely met. Could it be that I knew him less than I thought? I had been wondering why he had asked to stay with us when he always stayed with my parents. Maybe now, it was starting to make sense. Maybe he needed my help and he always knew he could rely on me to be there for him.

I prayed for wisdom and compassion and then got up to start a busy day of preparations. Vases of flowers were placed in their bedroom as Charlie and Sam raced around the house getting their toys ready to show the baby.

Getting Charlie and Sam to bed that night was a challenge. They were on camp beds in different rooms and highly excited. As soon as they were tucked up they leapt out again. They seemed to be everywhere waving Easter Chicken wildly and bursting through doors shouting "burrr" on behalf of Scotty bear. It must have taken two hours to get them to bed by which time I was well ready for a well-earned glass of wine which John kindly brought to me as I sank back on the sofa. Peace at last and jobs done. I was ready, tired, in pain, but content. All was quiet and my idea of a perfect evening was to lie and sip wine with John and say nothing, then go to bed early. As I finished my glass of wine, John, still drinking his, came and sat on the floor at the side of the sofa and held my hand. This was lovely, safe, and, considering the pain, as close to bliss as I would get.

"Pam" he whispered quietly, "Have you ever been tempted?"

"Of course," I laughed "Everyone is, what a silly question!"

"I was tempted once," he continued.

"Only once!" I chuckled. He had got off lightly!

"Yes," was a strange response and my amusement gradually changed to confusion as I realized that he was looking at the carpet instead of me.

There was silence.......then more silence......and more ... as I began to piece together what he was saying. With a chill the message of Every Day With Jesus came back to my mind. Adultery was right at the top of my unseen list of things I could not face in life. I felt as if that one thing would kill me. I would rather face John's death than that. My marriage was sacred to me and John knew from the start that adultery would be the end of our marriage. If this was what he was trying to say, I could not make sense of it. He knew what this would do to me and I did believe he loved me.

"You're not saying,"....... Was all I could get out.

"Yes, I know it is adultery," he muttered still looking at the floor.

Another long silence began as I tried to take it in.

Suddenly, the silence was broken but not by words. An invisible knife plunged from the ceiling and sharply pierced me through my breastbone pinning me to the back of the sofa. It was as sharp as if it was real and the physical pain it caused was real and excruciating.

John kept looking at the floor and I just sat as the thoughts passed through my head. I could never forgive adultery and John knew this meant divorce. But Jesus forgave the woman caught in adultery and I had no doubt he was asking me to forgive John. In my head I prayed, "I know you are asking me to forgive but I can't. I don't even want to forgive. But I want to obey and so I want to forgive. That is where I start and you're going to have to do something."

At that moment, I had no words for John. I handed him the open page I had read in the morning and he read the same, then the tears started to pour down his face. I had no feelings at all. All I felt was that this nightmare had immaculately bad timing. How was I going to be normal when Jim and Louise turned up in twenty-four hours?

I then began my automatic reaction to crisis. I had to know all the facts.

"You knew what this would do," I began. "Didn't you consider that?"

"I was the other side of the Atlantic," explained a broken John. "I thought there was no way you'd find out and so you'd never be hurt. I hadn't reckoned on Jesus. He's kept on and on at me to tell you. That's why I wanted to go to see Robert. I needed to ask him if you had to know but Jesus has just kept on at me. I knew today I had to tell you."

I needed all the facts right down to the most minute detail because that left no room for any untrue negatives to invade my imagination and knife me. Two hours of interrogation began. It was extremely uncomfortable for John, and each detail stuck the knife in further. I even needed to know the colour of the sheets.

"Did you not think that you might have caught some unpleasant disease?" I questioned. "Some of them have no symptoms in men and herpes is at the moment incurable in women? Did you not even care about my health?"

For a moment, I felt mildly angry at the stupidity and irresponsibility.

"I never thought," cried John, "It was just an adventure, an excitement."

So this is how much Charlie, Sam, and I mean to you, I thought.

When we had said all that could be said, I still had no feelings apart from a deep sadness and a feeling that I had failed. My best had not been good enough. I wanted to die. I went straight over to the cocktail cabinet and drank three quarters of a bottle of whisky and lay on the sofa waiting for the darkness to come and take me away from all the pain. It came and for a while I was spared what I could not take, but then I started to come round with the room spinning and as I tried to stop it by leaning sideways, I was violently sick all over the carpet. I was conscious of John putting a rug over me and thoughtfully placing a bucket beside me. I knew he was there all night as I slept and vomited my way through the next six hours.

A new day dawned as Charlie and Sam awoke to find us there. Mummy does not feel very well or very happy was an explanation that made complete sense to them. "Go to work!" I ordered John. I knew that while he was there I would not pull myself together. Without question he went and I have never seen anyone look such a mess. I had to make a plan but my head would not think so I decided I would take the day in small stages according to priority. Breakfast for the boys was the starting point. I sat with them and Scotty Bear rubbed his felt nose against mine with a compassionate "burrr" for someone not feeling well and Easter Chicken squeaked and danced up and down on the Shreddies until I put the milk on. Even they had no ability to irritate me today. Charlie and Sam were firmly, not gently, dressed in duffle coats with mittens with an attitude that said "we ARE going to get to school," and with supernatural determination we set off. How do you walk up a pavement holding two little hands with an enormous glass dome over you? It felt as if everyone was outside the dome. I could see mouths moving but heard no words. People were laughing and moving. It was as if I was in a real world and they were part of a play. As if an enormous earthquake had occurred and everyone apart from me was oblivious to it. I let go of Charlie and Sam's hands and they shot across the play-ground to their friends. I knew for a few hours they were safely away from all this and I made an about turn and retraced my steps in my glass case.

Once home, I sat and sipped my way through a cup of coffee and tried to sort out what to do. It was too late to cancel Jim's visit so to get ready for them needed to be the start and perhaps I could put this nightmare on hold. It was at this point that pain for once was my friend and not my enemy. I had learnt that when it was at its worst I could not think, so on easier days I made lists and plans that I could follow on automatic pilot on unbearable days. There were the lists telling me what to do and so all I had to do was fol-low them. Clean toilet, wash up breakfast, put clean towels for Jim and Louise, and thaw out gateau. Through the day, I followed the plan ending with another glass dome trip to collect the boys. When they entered the house, small signs reminded them that Jim was coming and they burst into a frenzy of excited activity. I sat and numbly watched. I had a big problem. This all had to be kept on hold and how could I fool Jim into thinking everything was normal? I did not want anyone to know. I did not want to admit my failure; I was a very proud and materialistic person. People say pride comes before a fall, but the Bible says pride goes before destruction and I was not too sure what was being destroyed, my pride or me! I was concerned for Louise. She is a gentle and sensitive person and she would easily pick up that something out of the ordinary was going on, and if she did not know, would probably think she had done something wrong. OH WHAT A NIGHTMARE.

Jim does not smile, he beams. He is always beaming. I think he is a sort of Cheshire cat and whatever happens to him all that will be left will be the beam! I do not know how we will recognize each other in our next life, but I think I will recognize that beam. The doorbell rang and in came the beam followed by Jim then Louise and the baby. Thankfully for me, Charlie and Sam were so excited that they were an excellent distraction for our visitors until they went to bed, but then a difficult decision had to be made. Pride had to take a blow as I chose to tell Jim what had happened. After all, he is my best friend. He was not a Christian and he knew a little of our experiences, but I was unsure of his reaction. When I look back, I think how silly I was to have even thought this way. When I told Jim his reaction was typical of him. He put a hand on my shoulder and just quietly and calmly said "Do you still love him because I do?" As Jim had demonstrated all his life, I saw instant forgiveness. How I wished I could catch some of it from him. The subject was closed and once Louise knew, she did what she could to help by offering to have me to stay if I needed space to think. It had seemed the worst timing in the world for this blow, but I know now how perfect that timing was because Jim and Louise just by being with us helped us through the difficult two days while my emotions were thawing out.

We visited the museum, played with the baby, and Jim and Louise thoughtfully took Charlie and Sam for games in the woods and occupied them. I was so grateful. After a busy Saturday, the children were all put to bed and I stared into space as John tried to keep normal conversation going. I hoped with a couple of glasses of wine in me, I would sleep but I woke at about two o clock in the morning with an enormous jolt as I realized that the nightmare was real. I started to get very distressed. John had wisely told Chris what had happened and he phoned him. The faithful Chris got out of bed and dressed and came round to pray. I was horrified. Because Jim and Louise were in the boy's room, we had all the washing in our room. If Chris came up he would see THE WASHING!! People of any worth just did not have washing in their bedrooms! Oh the humiliation of it all! I heard Chris come up the stairs and it was more than I could take so I stood at the top of the stairs and shouted at him " GO AWAY, CHRIS YOU ARE NOT WANTED!"

He got the message quickly and beat a hasty retreat down the stairs to the lounge where he sat and prayed with John. What on earth Jim and Louise were making of all of this, I hated to imagine. Chris had been quite frustrated that he had not been able to move up north with the others, but as usual, when we look back, we can see God's perfect timing. We needed Chris at this time and were going to need him increasingly in the weeks ahead. We owe him for eternity, a deep debt of gratitude.

With love and hugs, we said goodbye to Jim and his family and then had to get on with dealing with the situation. Our priority was to try and keep things as normal as possible for the boys and we decided to tell as few people as possible. Jesus had told me to forgive and for me it was humanly impossible, I realized that the last thing I needed was people's emotional opinions and the input of anyone who would pull me the other way. This marriage had to somehow come through this. I really did believe that John was truly repentant but forgiveness would not come nor could I trust. We did not know where to start.

Chapter 10

A New Start

Let us go back to the beginning seemed a good starting place. We would go back to before we were married. As John went to open the front door on his way to work, I took off my wedding ring and engagement ring and handed them back to him then walked back to the kitchen without saying a word. I watched as he crestfallenly put them into a little plastic wallet used for work samples and placed them in his jacket pocket and then he left. He did not know if this meant divorce and I am not sure whether I did either. I swung between divorce and staying together with unnerving rapidity. I knew what God wanted, but I was crying out for justice. The presence of Charlie and Sam made the decisions all the more agonizing. I was determined to obey Jesus but had no idea how.

At the end of a long day, John unusually went to bed before me and for some reason that I still do not know was lying on my side of the bed. I stood and looked at him and felt such an overwhelming love for this man. I wanted him to comfort me in my pain and yet it was him who had caused the pain. It was such a dilemma. The love inside of me was like a mountain but from deep within it burst a volcano eruption of totally unexpected pain, closely followed by such a raging murderous anger that poured up through my chest, down my arm, and into my hand. It turned my hand into a tight fist that hit John across the jaw with a force that I could not have imagined, throwing him sideways into the bedside table and knocking over the light.

I took a step backwards and stood and observed the scene in front of me. Who did that? That could not have been me. I do not behave like that. I don't know who was more shocked, John or I. Apart from a cut he was not seriously damaged and as he sat up came out with the amazing statement, "That hurt!"

I should think it did! I was horrified. How could I do that to the man I loved? Where was forgiveness in this? In bewildered shock, I fell across his chest, burying my head in his pyjamas, and sobbing my heart out whilst he stroked my hair. We lay quiet, both thinking the same unvoiced thoughts. What is going to happen to us? I asked John to forgive me and then we prayed together a simple "help!" prayer. Then we started to plan.

The starting point we decided was to sell my engagement ring. It was always a source of sadness to me. My mother had been adamantly against our engagement or marriage and I had to fight for two years before she gave in and allowed us to get engaged. It all happened when John was away on a work training course. She invited round a friend from the jewellery trade and without asking or even mentioning it to John asked him to make me an engagement ring. The friend brought round a selection of stones and settings and I sat and explained what I wanted. At every stage, I was given a good reason why what I wanted was not right. I wanted a little sapphire but was told "No, you must have a diamond so it will match with any colour outfit and also it will be saleable when you need to sell it!" I think I was just so relieved to at last be able to get engaged that I would have settled for any ring, but I ended up with a ring almost identical to my mother's and a deep sadness that I never went to a little shop and chose a little cheaper ring with John. It was like getting engaged to my mother!

Well, now the words were wise. We had an expensive diamond to sell. John took some hours off work next day and we went to a reputable jeweller and sold the ring. In its place we bought a new white gold wedding ring and a white gold eternity ring with five stones on it. A central diamond for Jesus, two sapphires either side for John and me and two little diamonds at each end for Charlie and Sam. John's parents came up from Devon to look after the boys for a weekend and we went to the Cotswolds. Inside a large empty vast church, two small figures sat away from the world making new vows to each other and to Jesus, unseen by people but joined by God. It was not the traditional Anglican vows we had made twelve years before but private sincere ones heard by us and God, with whose help we shall keep.

An ecstatic Sam burst through the door on our return announcing that Grandma had cooked lamb and mint sauce. We were all smiling and happy but deep inside the wounds were too painful to express for either of us. New rings gave a new beginning and a start but we were to need so much help and desperately needed that job up north. Still, no matter how we tried neither Chris nor John could move so we clung onto them.

With each new day, the physical and emotional pain continued unbearably. I thought the facial pain was in some ways easier to bear. We tried to protect the boys from our feelings and I still do not know how well we succeeded. We did our best. In the house, I just felt pain, but as soon as I walked through the door into the outside world, the glass dome covered me. I felt in a different world from everyone else.

Inside the house, a worrying new problem started. If I looked at John I felt such enormous love for him and that was quickly followed, even before I could realize it, by such hurt and betrayal that anger and violence took over and I started hitting John. At first it was a minor slap, but it began to escalate into tight-fisted blows. Something in me wanted him to hurt as much as I was hurting. As I tried to pull myself together, I found that the physical pain was compounding the problem. Instead of hurling myself around the room hitting my head on the walls, I turned the energy into hitting, scratching, and biting John. I really did want to forgive and I kept praying for Jesus to help me, but it just got worse. Chris was a tremendous support to John in those days and John amazed me that he never hit back. He developed an art of restraining me. I suppose any sensible person would have turned to the doctor in this situation, but we and the fellowship were confident that God would bring us through. In an ever increasing state of distress, I was regularly carted up north where the Elders of the fellowship advised John and prayed with us. Prayer seemed to make it even worse and my behaviour became more and more unacceptable and bizarre. I started to have terrifying dreams involving figures with unnatural faces and bodies and John soon learned that if he heard me whimpering in the night, I was in my dreams screaming my head off and then he woke me and comforted me. It was all getting more than I could take and I begged John to get me into hospital. However, the church leaders were sure the problem was spiritual and that Jesus was the only way we would solve it. A hospital could only sedate me. At times, I could function normally and at those times I made it my priority to try to keep life secure and stable for Charlie and Sam but then I would unexpectedly swing into violence but always John was there for them because it was the sight of him that triggered the change. With the faithful Chris beside us, we adopted a policy of telling no one. The intention was to keep the family together and the involvement of "professionals" would have probably meant the boys being either sent to my parents, whose involvement in their upbringing we were trying to keep to a minimum, or being taken into care. However, the church leaders felt that they were in no danger and I in my rational moments could guarantee their safety. The people in danger were John and me, him from murder and me from suicide. I had taken more than I could bear.

One night, we were clinging onto each other in bed and reviewing the previous two days. John said, "One day, Pam, we'll laugh about this." Now we do and we would never have thought that it would be recorded in a book to amuse the rest of the world. John had been invited to a works dinner and asked if I felt well enough for him to leave us. I did not like him going out without me, but I had to start to trust him and I agreed. We both put Charlie and Sam to bed and then John changed, kissed me goodbye, and left. I was in bed drowsy when he returned and all that I was aware of was a phenomenal waft of garlic all over me.

"What on earth have you been eating?" I gasped.

"Garlic," was the reply that brought with it an even greater waft. Suddenly, I changed to the other Pam and kicked John out of bed ferociously and leapt out myself to pursue him down the stairs. He was now wise to this and knew he was in for a beating and bolted through the front door shutting it behind him. I stomped back to bed and lay waiting to see what would happen. I do not think I actually thought at times like that. I acted on instinct. The next event was Charlie getting out of bed. "Why have you got up, Charlie?"

I asked gently. "Daddy's throwing stones at my window," he explained sleepily,

"I think he wants me to let him in." I held his hand as we went down the stairs and we let Daddy in. We took Charlie back to bed and I kissed John and then we both kissed Charlie who quickly went back to sleep. We got wearily back into bed and then John made the grave mistake of treating me to another gassing with garlic. It speedily produced exactly the same reaction as before but faster. As John bolted through the door, I put down the little knob on the lock so there was no way he could get in. Back in bed, after a few minutes, in walked Charlie disgruntly complaining "He's doing it again." I wanted to protect Charlie from the seriousness of the situation and thought of the best way I could to give him peace. I lied!

"It's a dream, Charlie," I lied and tucked him up in my bed and stroked his hair until he went to sleep.

With no keys to the house or garage, John was left in the porch in his pyjamas. The full amusement to everyone involved that night was the type of pyjamas that John liked to wear. They are not made now and the best way I can describe them is that they were like adult beige babygrows! Not the best apparel for an October night. John's great gifting is problem solving and he definitely had a problem. He also had his green wellies that were kept in the porch and so with no other option, he put them on and jogged the 500 yards to Chris, dressed in his babygrows and wellies. A sleepy and gob-smacked Chris let him in and trying to stifle the hysterical laughter that he could feel welling up inside attempted to get his head around the seriousness of the situation. He made John up the sofa bed where John spent the night being kept awake by the never-ending laughter of Chris and his wife in the room above.

It was the most miserable night I can remember. I desperately wanted John home but something inside me would not have it. In the morning, Charlie and Sam presumed that Daddy had gone to work and went to school blissfully unaware of anything more than a strange night. I wanted John back but could not overcome this unidentifiable opposition to my true desires. I prayed and prayed and then God solved the dilemma in a way only he could have thought of. He allowed to happen something that he knew I could not handle alone. I have always been terrified of feathers and in the morning a blackbird flew into the patio door and lay either stunned or injured on the concrete. Poor thing. I could not leave it to suffer but I also could not go near it. As John had no choice the previous night, I had no choice but to swallow my pride and phone Chris to see if he would help me find John. The only response I got from Chris was an outburst of laughter. Funnily enough, the week before John had lent Chris a suit to attend an interview for a job to enable him to move and they were exactly the same size. This time John returned wearing Chris's jeans and jumper and the blackbird was saved and the family reunited. John promised that we would laugh about this and every so often we do.

We and the church leaders knew our situation was desperate and everyone had fasted and prayed. The leaders were convinced my problem was spiritual. They had been learning a lot from the teachings and experiences of a wonderful Bible teacher called Derek Prince and were learning all about demons (or evil spirits) and the devil. We read about how Jesus cast evil spirits out of people who were controlled by them or possessed, and how he restored peace and brought healing. John and I both now had personal experience of the Holy Spirit at work in our lives today. We had been constantly amazed at the power in the name of Jesus and the peace and healing that the Holy Spirit brought to give glory to Jesus and to build the Kingdom of God. All this teaching, however, about the devil and demons and a spiritual war was completely new to us. I am not sure how new this was to the leaders up north, but they believed that this was a work that the Holy Spirit wanted to do in that particular time. I am just overwhelmingly grateful to God for putting us with these people as God worked in them. It was the perfect place at the perfect time. God knew better than we did what was wrong and was about to keep his promise to help us although at the time it seemed so hopeless. The leaders believed that my problem was caused by a demon and that Jesus would deliver me. We had not a clue but trusted them and were prepared to give it a shot. We had nothing to lose and nowhere else to go.

We pinned our hopes on a visit to the fellowship from a team of Christians from Belfast. They claimed that they were experiencing a powerful work of the Holy Spirit and were seeing miracle healings and people set free from demons.

They claimed that one man who had undergone a failed operation was not only healed, but his operation scar had disappeared. People were so amazed that they signed an affidavit confirming the fact. You choose whether to believe them or not. We knew the power of the Holy Spirit and we knew he was capable of anything he wanted to do to glorify Jesus and so we chose to believe them.

A weekend was arranged at a place by the sea called Kinmel Hall, and there was very high expectation that as we got together with these people miracles would occur. Faith was high and everyone was excited. We were in too much of a mess to get excited. It was our main aim to just get there. In

our desperation, it was our last hope. I made John promise
that if God did nothing, he would get me into hospital as
soon as we came home.

The three weeks before that weekend were unending.
I regularly swung from being myself to being violent. I
wanted to die. John was covered in bites, scratches, and
bruises, and we were still desperately trying to hold things
together for Charlie and Sam. Chris was invaluable and
gave us way beyond what an ordinary friend would. He
gave everything to get us through, even going as far as
taking a day off work to propel me round the supermarket
and make sure we had food. A lot of what went on I cannot remember, but I do remember holding onto his coat
as we went round behind the shopping trolley. I had not
a clue what to buy. I was in my glass dome and there was
nothing in my head. Chris picked things up off the shelves
and put them in the trolley. I still do not know who paid. I
might owe him a bit!! Those weeks we did not starve and
Charlie and Sam had a regular supply of baked beans and
chocolate biscuits and so they were happy. You might think
us irresponsible but we kept no secrets from Charlie and
Sam. John taught them as we learned, in a simple honest
way. He explained who Jesus is and about the devil being
our enemy. He told them that Mummy was poor and that
we believed that Jesus would make me better and prepared
them for the visit to Kinmel Hall. It was a help that Chris,
Derek, and Terry, all had children the same age who were
being taught the same things, and we all got together to find
the best ways to teach the children. The sort of understanding the children had was demonstrated clearly by the boys
as we walked up to school.

"Charlie. Will there be lamb and mint sauce in Heaven?"
queried Sam

"I expect so," replied Charlie with a tone of authority.

"I want to go there now!" enthused Sam.

"Well you can't," concluded Charlie. "You've got some devil fighting to do first!"

A child's words, but how simple and true. They had grasped that Christianity is more than just hymns and hats and flowers. It is a war.

Two weeks before we went to Kinmel Hall, I had the nightmare above all nightmares. If I could have seen ahead two weeks, I would have taken it as an encouragement that God was on the case, but at the time it absolutely terrified me. I was getting uncomfortably used to dreaming of terrible demonic figures and was just so grateful when John woke me up and it was just a dream. This dream was a little different in that it was detailed and specific. I dreamt that I was standing in front of a long wooden desk behind which were 3 people. The nearest description I can find is that of a courtroom. The people behind the desk I recognized as having some form of authority, rather like judges. They asked what I wanted and I said I wanted to be free from violence and suicide and other things that I could not name. The judges discussed this and then I found myself on top of a piano keyboard dancing with VERY fast feet. That does not sound frightening, but in the dream it was absolutely petrifying. I then saw a white eerie figure that had a slimy feel about it. I was whimpering so much that I woke John and he woke me, only for the dream to continue as soon as I went back to sleep. I fell off the keyboard and started biting everything around me. The dream seemed unending. Since that night, no one will ever be able to convince me that there is no such place as hell. It was an enormous relief to wake up even though I was beginning another day of severe pain and total unpredictability.

The day before we went to Kinmel Hall, I amazed myself by being able to pack and I even had a little time for myself before school fetching time. I decided to take a walk round the block to get a bit of fresh air and distract myself from our situation. As I walked, the awfulness of it all would not leave me. So many emotions were running wild in my head and above all I felt so so angry. Who was I angry with? Was it John? What he did hurt so much and yet did it warrant such anger? Was it myself? I felt I had failed and yet I had done my best. Was it God? Well it was not his fault. We cannot blame him for our mistakes and sins. Was it the other woman? Yes, to an extent. I found her actions hard to understand. As I turned the corner to walk past the Anglican Church, I realized who I was so angry with. It was Satan, the devil himself. He was the one who deserved the anger and as I saw the church doors open for visitors I decided to go in and give him a piece of my mind. I looked at the blue and white ceiling and then down at the blue carpet. I had only been in here once before. I glanced around to make sure there was no one there and then I stood in front of the altar and let forth a torrent of abuse. I screamed "How dare he try to destroy our marriage! How dare he try to kill and torment me. How dare he try to break up our family and rob us." I then raged on ferocious warnings to the devil at a hundred decibels that Jesus was far more powerful than he, that he had been defeated on the cross by Jesus and that he would pay for all he had tried to do to us!" I raged at him on and on until I ran out of raging and words and energy and stood gasping for breath and staring at the altar. There was complete silence. I waited not knowing what for. The silence was interrupted by a little rustle at the side of the church and to my horror from behind a portable screen emerged a terrified cowering verger who held a large book in front of himself as if in defence and said in a whisper "Can I help you?"

"Nn..no," I stuttered in my embarrassment and shuffled out backwards as the greatly relieved man continued his duties. As I walked back to the school to fetch the boys, I wondered what that did to that man. Would he ever find himself in a situation as desperate and bizarre as ours and would he ever understand what was going on that day?

Chapter 11

War!

It was Friday. We only had to make it through this day to get there. We had a plan. John would take me and the boys to a friend to make sure we were safe and then go to work. It was not easy and I remember trying so hard to appear as if everything was alright when it clearly was not. I had known Ellie well and she has said since how worried she was that day but I have never been able to tell her what it was all about. The plan worked and the boys had a happy day playing with Ellie's girls and we were collected at five o'clock by John who was not at all looking forward to the journey. It would take three hours at best and the occupying of Charlie and Sam was a minor problem compared with the distinct possibility that he would be punched on the side of his head as he was driving. The fact that John has no sight in one eye made it worse because he could not look ahead and see me at the same time and so protect himself from the blows.

Everyone knew our situation. We were notorious by then and so everyone was praying for our protection. It was dark when we arrived tired and relieved but the battle was not ended but only just begun.

Today, I sometimes wish I could go to Kinmel Hall to see exactly what it looks like as I was so ill when we arrived. It seemed a depressing place to me but I am sure the pitch darkness did not help that. It was a very large old building and appeared isolated amongst a small forest of trees which lead their way to the hall through a windy bumpy lane. In the blackness, the front of the building was illuminated by some form of exterior lighting and so John dropped me off outside the front door, with Charlie and Sam and our bags.

"Is this where Jesus will make Mummy better?" asked Sam, his little neck craned back in order to see the roof so high up.

"We hope so," I answered as a prayer.

I could not face going in. For the past week, fear had been beyond belief and I was terrified. We waited for John, and I shivered as I looked at the enormous heavy wooden doors. They needed to be large and heavy for what looked the equivalent of a stately home, but why were they wavery and distorted just as were the windows? It was eerie and I did not want to go in. John soon appeared and took two small hands and let us in, with me holding onto his coat. I was not going to let go. If he was there, I was safe. The brightness hit me like a wall and made me blink my eyes as we walked in. It was such a contrast with the darkness outside. It seemed a million people were milling around in the entrance hall. They were (I now know) being allocated rooms, but it felt like a railway station and the noise was deafening. I put down the bags and then every mother's nightmare began as I realized that John had let go of Sam in order to sign a form and we had lost him in the crowd. Charlie was gone too and I could not move through the masses to find them. Everyone there apart from the team from Belfast knew us and why we were there, and I just prayed that someone would be watching out for them and looking after them. When we were allocated our rooms, we went to look for them and found that, hand in hand, they had made their way into a large side room, which was empty and had found, to their delight, a snooker table and they were happily playing with the balls. Chris had already installed his family and came and promised to keep a look out for the boys and take them to a nearby beach with his children on Saturday to give us all the time and freedom we could have.

With John, I felt safe but the next problem began when I was told that they had put him in a men's dormitory and me and the boys in a ladies' dormitory. With the terrifying nightmares and the violence and pain I dare not be separated from him through the night. It would not be wise or considerate to the other ladies. They could not handle my situation. They did not have the experience of living with me. We voiced our concern but were told that no arrangements were to be changed. (Afterwards we learned that they wanted the problems to really surface so they would know what they were dealing with, and surface the problems did!!) I went absolutely berserk, hurling myself around and screaming. John put into practice his art of restraining and the leaders gave us a little room at the top of a long windy staircase to be by ourselves and to settle me down. The fear was overwhelming, I was shaking all over and I could not see properly. There was to be an introductory meeting that evening and so we left to put the boys to bed. As we stood at the top of the huge staircase, I steadied myself by putting my right hand on the wooden bannister and looked down. At the bottom of the stairs, I could identify above the others the tall, dignified, authoritative figure of Colin. I had only dared to speak to him once. He seemed as far above me as God himself and he was well aware that we were there but he could not see us. He stood far below us at the bottom of the stair, directing people and sorting their problems. I made the fatal mistake of thinking that I did not want to be there and then, remembering the sleeping arrangements, gave John a well aimed kick in the back that took him completely unaware and sent him hurtling and rolling from the top to the bottom where he landed at the feet of Colin.

I stood with my hands over my mouth and my eyes as big as saucers as I took in the consequence of my action. John did not move. Colin looked down at him in shock and then, to my horror, up at me. I was identified as the cause of this! Before I could run he came sprinting up the stairs although it was all happening in slow motion for me. What would he do to me? As a child, I was well used to a good hard belt across the head for being naughty but that was only for little things and this man was nearly God. What punishment could I expect for something as bad as this? Rooted to the spot with hands over my ears I shut my eyes and waited for the first shout or blow. A strong, firm hand pulled my hand off my right ear and a gentle voice asked "Are you alright?" Was this man mad? Was I alright? What about John? He might be dead for all I knew. No one had ever cared for me in this way before. With tears streaming down my face, he led me down to where a group of people were helping up John and then they took us straight to our seats in the meeting room. No words were said. We just looked at one another in despair. A lady I had never met came and told us that Charlie and Sam were in bed and not to worry about them. They were being cared for.

We looked as the team from Belfast assembled on the stage and then started to sing some worship choruses. I could not sing. There was absolutely nothing to sing about. One chorus contained many promises of God to heal and save and deliver being given thanks for by the songwriter who had experienced them. I could see no point in singing it so I just stood, but Oh No!! Colin from his exalted place on the stage could see I was not singing and was making his way off the

stage and down to tell me off. There was no way to run out.
I was on the end, but he would get to me before I could get
out. I cringed against John and waited for the rebuke. The
tall figure stooped to the level of my ear and then whispered,
"One day you will be able to sing all this and know it to be
true for you." I was beyond being amazed. How he demonstrated God's love and comfort and forgiveness to me. At my
least lovable, he had picked me out of the crowd and set me
apart to love me. The tears continued to pour.

Half an hour later, the speaker began his introduction.
All the names in this book have been changed but I want
to name the Irish people. I cannot contact them and twenty
years on have no idea what has happened to them, but I
would like to think that one day, maybe, they might read
this book and know what an enormous debt of gratitude
we owe them as they came to help us at great personal cost.
The speaker was Jim Quinn. He talked about how Christians
could have problems with demons, why this can happen,
and how to get rid of them. He then opened the meeting
up for questions. We looked at our watches as he began his
question time and guessed that he must have spoken for half
an hour. He had in fact been speaking for over two hours,
but the time just flew. We were fascinated. He was putting
Jesus's work of deliverance in the Bible into today for us. It
is happening now and we had hope. At Christmas, we sing
Emmanuel (Meaning God with us) and he really is!

There were many questions. Some people could not
accept that a Christian could have this problem. We, however, knew without a doubt that we had a problem and
before I headed to the psychiatric hospital we wanted to
give God a chance. Before the end of the questions, some
unhappy people left to pack their bags, but we chose to stay.
We had nothing to lose and John had always said, as he
regularly does in a bad time, "Lets judge it at the end."

We had expected that the questions would end the evening and as it was ten o'clock were ready for bed, but Jim was ready to begin. He started to proclaim the power and authority of the blood of Jesus and everyone jolted as a woman at the back of the room let out a bloodcurdling scream. An Irish team member sprinted to her aid and then the room seemed to disintegrate into chaos as team members leapt over empty seats to shrieking, howling people who had ended up on the floor. I grabbed John's hand in my terror and then let it go and ran. I raced as fast as I could for the front door, pushing open its great weight, and charged out across the car park into the trees where I hid. I had no idea where John would be and hoped he would come and look for me and find me. From behind the tree I could see the large wooden doors and I fixed my eyes on them and prayed for him to come. If God heard that prayer, He certainly did not answer. I concluded that we cannot make God do anything. No one came.

Did anybody care? I was now shaking with fear and also with cold. After all it was November. Should I go back in? It just was not an option. From my hiding place I could still hear the shrill sounds of demons disappearing through the windows and into the air and the howling. Back in there? Oh no!

Then in a rational moment, I remembered that I still had the car keys in my pocket. That was what I would do. Crouching down I made my way to the car, let myself in, and lay down and hid behind the back seat. In the distance the noise went on and on. I was cold but better in the car than outside. I was safe and gradually the fear subsided. By midnight, I had resigned myself to not seeing John and I wondered what had happened to him. I knew Charlie and Sam were safe and tomorrow we would go home and then I could go to hospital. There was no chance of going to sleep in this ridiculous position, so I waited for the dawn to come. I did not have to wait that long. In

another ten minutes, I heard the car keys in the lock and knew
there was only one person who they were with. John had found
me. Oh the relief! Safe at last, I could move into the front and
sit down. John held me and rubbed my cold hands and warmed
me and then asked me to go in. The fear began shaking me
again and I pleaded to go home. Calmly, John understood that
I was too scared to be away from him, but he was insistent that
we stay. "People are getting healed in there," he stated. "I know
it's not nice but here, Pam, we do have a chance. Please stick it
through the weekend. Judge it at the end."

"Will you take me to hospital on Monday?" I bargained.

"Yes, if I need to," he promised. We needed to be
together that night and so we put the seats as far back as we
could and then, leaning across the gear stick, we cuddled
and amazingly, we slept.

Dawn broke and cramped but rested I slunk back into the
Hall propped up by John. Chris was on his way to the seaside
with Charlie, Sam, and his children. We took our seats and
punctually Jim Quinn began with worship and teaching. He
read the end of the part of the Bible telling of Jezebel and her
horrendous death. He talked about a spirit of Jezebel and some
of the problems it caused. I did not know one end of the Bible
from the other and this was double dutch to me. In preparation for the weekend, I learned the fellowship had been taught
all about this in depth because it had been identified as a major
problem, but as we were away from them we knew nothing
and it meant nothing to me. All I could say was when the
name Jezebel was mentioned, I felt a physical thump on my
chest. As Jim read the closing passage about Jezebel's death,
before he had had time to pray, our dustman's wife let out the
loudest scream I have ever heard and then again there were
people all over the place praying with people and the greatest
commotion I have ever witnessed. I was not over-alarmed this
time and just coldly and without emotion observed it all.

I did not feel much like lunch and the burnt omelette did nothing to whet my appetite. Whilst I sat next to Derek's wife, I asked her all about Jezebel. It had bothered me. "Lots of us have had a problem with this," she explained as if it was an everyday thing. I was surprised at her calm. I told her what I felt and she gave me a quick instruction course on the subject, concluding with the concerning comment that she would not be at all surprised if it was part of my problem but that Jesus would not deliver a person from a demon until they knew how it used them because once a demon has gone you have to learn to break the bad habits it has caused or it can get back in again and cause trouble all over again.

Oh well … we shall see.

Charlie and Sam made a brief appearance at lunch to delight in the fun they had enjoyed on the beach and to voice their disgust at the standard of the food! Armed with money for ice cream, they went away and we returned to the afternoon session. I was losing the fear and began to feel a flicker of hope. Then I had a surprise. In walked Charlie and Sam. We had told them beforehand what would be happening, but I was very concerned because nothing would have prepared any of us for the dramatic deliverances.

"Why have you brought them in?" I asked Chris

"It's because this bit is for the children," he replied.

I was not at all sure that this was wise. This was not children's stuff and I thought it could cause them distress, but John wanted them there. The children's prayer time was so quiet and gentle. Jesus loves children and goes as far as to tell us to be like them (something I could never understand until Charlie taught me why a few years later). I found children quite a pain!

Two of the leaders came to pray for Charlie and Sam. They explained that God had a prophecy for them. A prophecy is a glimpse of their future. The Bible tells us to keep away from fortune tellers ... they go in the naughty bag, but sometimes the Holy Spirit will give a glimpse of the future. We have Charlie and Sam's prophecy on tape and twenty years on it has amazed me as it has come about in their lives with such accuracy. It said, God had a special job for Charlie and that he would give him the ability to work with the Holy Spirit in order to do things that other people could not do and that he would not become proud. It said that Sam would always have to wait for his prayers to be answered and that Jesus would never let him down. Sam still hates the waiting! It continued to say that they would be more than just blood brothers and that they would live far apart from each other in the world but would always be in contact and able to pray for each other accurately and specifically. Today Sam flits between London, America, and Singapore and Charlie is in Australia. They are in constant contact and their relationship gives me deep satisfaction. Charlie listened to the tape for the last time before he left for Australia. I feel God has so privileged him.

Still, back to the weekend. The children all left and then the deliverance continued in what to me seemed utter chaos. All unbearable noise and activity. There was no hype, but I was beginning to wonder if it was mass hysteria. Nothing was happening to me. It was me who needed healing and I knew God knew that. They were making it happen I thought until to my horror, the usually dignified John who headed up major presentations at work and had said "Don't expect me to get excited about this," to Chris and Derek collapsed in a heap on the floor. A young Irish man leapt to his side and began praying and as I watched in disgust at John frothing at the mouth and spitting, more people gathered round to praise God. I watched rooted to the floor and stunned. If this disgusting sight was John, this was real.

"Aren't you pleased? This is your husband God is healing," asked a stranger.

I was not pleased. I was disgusted and in any case how dare God heal John. He had caused me so much pain and he did not deserve it. Could not God see it was me needing healing, me in agony, me in distress? Perhaps I had had my rations from God. Perhaps he had given up on me. An embarrassed John sat up wiping his mouth on a handkerchief and I wanted nothing to do with him. It was disgusting. I did not find out until the following week that Jesus had cast out of John a demon of lust and adultery. Thank you SO much, Jesus. Hopefully John will continue to follow you and we will never have to go through such pain again. So this is what it is all about. The battle against Satan that Jesus won on the cross was not a piece of history but is applicable and oh so relevant in our lives. This is why I am writing this book. If people can know this they could be saved so much pain and suffering. In the last two months, two houses have gone up for sale. Two families have been broken up. It need not be. It breaks Jesus' heart and mine.

The events of the previous hour had greatly increased John's hope for me but my hope was almost gone. God had forgotten me. I chose to look forward to Monday. I had not had a wash or a meal since Friday morning. I would have a bubble bath and a Chinese takeaway.

Everyone was well aware of our desperation and baffled as to why God seemed to be doing nothing. They, with the best of intentions, tried to find out what the hold up was. I was repeatedly asked to acknowledge that I was a sinner. I got totally cheesed off with it but repeated the fact whilst shutting off my emotions. It did not matter any more. They tried verbal discipline, which annoyed me even more. They questioned me for unbelief and lack of faith, which infuriated me.

John was very disappointed and worried for me, but our friends plus his personal experience kept him going with the encouragement of all who knew us.

I went to bed in despair at a lower point than I think I have ever reached and longed for home. In the night, I woke and was hit with fear. I needed John. I crawled out of bed and then could not stand up so I crawled on my hands and knees to the men's dormitory and found him in a bottom bunk. I crawled into his bed and he helped me back onto my legs and back to my room saying "Hang on, Pam. We've not finished yet."

In the morning, I was totally numb. I was not interested in this anymore. Let us go home. However, our friends were still desperately praying but even John's hope died as we watched the men from Ireland pack their bags and put them on the bottom of the stairs and prepare to catch their plane.

I put on my coat and as I turned to leave, Colin stopped me and said, "They will pray once more for you before you go."

They took me to a little private room and eight men including John stood round me. There was no shouting, no hype. Someone whispered in my ear "In Jesus name I command you to name yourself." Nothing was said. I had nothing to say. I could think of nothing. I was ready to get up and leave, but a gentle hand rested on my shoulder and someone said "stay."

"It's no good," I pleaded, "There's nothing there. It's all nothingness."

A young man called Terry Koch said "I think it's insanity we've got here."

"Go for it," was the response.

Some men started praising Jesus, some prayed in tongues and the leader took authority over the spirit of insanity in Jesus' name and commanded it to go. Nothing happened and

I thought "this is a jumble sale." Then someone told me to take a deep breath, which I did. I felt something catch under my diaphragm and as I breathed out a shrill whining squeal rushed up my chest and out of my mouth and gradually faded away into thin air. IT HAD GONE!! Oh the relief and the peace. We all got on our knees and thanked Jesus. I was more grateful than I can express and I was ready to go but they had not finished and wanted to continue. They prayed against Jezebel and the demon left and as it did so my feet ran very fast just as in the dream. Now, I could see how the nightmare was connected. I was also freed from a spirit of frigidity (which was greatly to help our marriage) and as I fell on the floor and started biting at the ankles of the nearest person, a spirit of violence left with a nasty cackle. Everyone was amazed at the power of God. Since that day, I have never experienced something so overwhelming. We were very privileged to have been there and although I would never want to go through that experience again, I long to see God's power so strong again.

The team from Belfast left with their bags as if it was just any other weekend and we left more ecstatic than I have ever felt. That overwhelming love filled us again and the beauty all around us seemed so enhanced. Golden leaves in the sunlight gently fell on the car as we drove along the long drive to set off for home. On the way, we passed two of the leaders from the fellowship who were unaware of what had happened to us and were so concerned for us. We gave them a thumbs up as we passed and they could not miss the joy on our faces. I was sane and in my right mind and so at peace. All visual distortion had gone and my mental clarity had returned. What a powerful mighty loving God we have. Yes, I was still in pain but we could return together to rebuild our marriage and bring up our sons and fit into the plan that God had ahead for us.

Chapter 12

Freedom?

"What a contrast," I thought to myself as the car containing our little family made its way home that golden autumn Sunday afternoon. Terror, fear, despair, and uncertainty had filled the car as we had travelled to Wales only two days before, and a very different car load was returning home. I could not claim that the car was filled with peace. Charlie and Sam, who seemed oblivious to the enormity of what had happened, were predictably tormenting one another with Easter Chicken and Scotty Bear, accompanied by the familiar challenging sounds of "Burrr"...... Twenty years later, when asked about their memories of that special weekend, all they seemed to remember was a large snooker table!

The front seats held two much quieter occupants as John and I tried to take in the events of the weekend. One total disaster turned into one enormous victory at the last minute. John was right. "Let's judge it at the end." All I could feel was that indescribable feeling that I remembered so well from my walk back from Chris's house. Passion mingled with peace. I could see clearly, think clearly, and reflect. John could concentrate on the driving without any fear for our safety whilst, at the same time, wonder at what God had done for us. We knew something major was wrong with me but insanity was the last thing anyone of us would have concluded. How amazing that God knew exactly what was wrong and would choose to tell a young man who was listening intently to Him and who had the guts to speak out what he heard in faith. It was almost beyond belief. We know that the Bible tells many times of how Jesus cast demons out of people, but that He is still doing so today takes my breath away. Not only that but He would choose to do that for us in our desperation. What a God!

I puzzled as to why I had the problem with insanity and I did not have to think for long before understanding. I only had to look back a few generations in my family to see that it was an inherited problem that I had wrestled with all my life and overcome in my own strength until the time when the pressures were too great to prevent it from surfacing. It is so sad that so many people suffer through no fault of their own and try, as I had, to deal with their problems on their own when such a mighty powerful and all-knowing God could overcome for them, if they would let him. I suppose, like us, they have to try everything until they run out of options and there is nowhere and no one else to turn to. It has to come to the choice: Jesus or die.

"We were free!" "We were free!" We were free and yet that did not mean that we were free from all our problems. We were free to return home and face them clear-headedly with Jesus. We were advised as we left to find a good local church for help and support until God made our move to the fellowship possible. Our car carried four people and four boxes containing problems. The first box contained my illness. Though sane, I was still in constant severe pain that was gradually invading all of my body from my head through my pelvis and into my legs. The second box contained John's search for a new job so that we could join the others up north. The third box contained Charlie's forthcoming spinal surgery, and the last box contained rebuilding our marriage and, in a way, getting to know each other all over again.

As I turned to request that Easter Chicken and Scotty Bear should lower their volume, I was aware that a few miles behind us Chris would be following us home. He was out of sight but it was a warm and comfortable feeling to know that we were not alone. He had his own problems, but only one problem box in his car. His contained the problem of selling his house so that he could move. He was nearer moving to join the others, but the house was just not selling. We knew that he was as much overcome with awe and amazement as to all that had happened to us and to others. We needed a church to support us, but who would believe us if we tried to tell them of our experiences? My mind pondered over the various local churches, and I was rapidly concluding that there was no where to go. We had to stick close to Chris and take it a little at a time.

The woods were shrouded in darkness as we drew near to home and the red "For Sale" sign outside Chris's house shouted at us as we passed. All was silence in our car as Easter Chicken and Scotty Bear had exhausted their owners and Charlie and Sam had drifted off to sleep, their heads rolling towards each other as they slept. It was an easy job to gently carry them out of the car and undress them, ready for bed. They hardly woke and were soon tucked up in bed, leaving us too tired to unpack or even speak. Too tired for the greatly desired and promised bubble bath, I clambered into bed and snuggled against John. I put my arms around his warm, curled-up body and as we allowed our minds to wander silently through our private memories of an incredible weekend, we drifted off to sleep, content to leave the future in God's hands.

The alarm clock signalled the start of a new day. It appeared no different from any other day and as I walked down the hill, having taken Charlie and Sam to school, it could have been any other day except for the awareness that we had experienced something so extraordinary. We were so privileged and the direction of our lives so changed. It was too much to take in. I unlocked the front door and cast my eyes over the debris that had been abandoned the night before. Coats were dumped on the floor and half-opened cases waited to be unpacked, but my heart was not in dealing with these practical necessities. I needed space to reflect on our weekend and try to grasp some vision of the future. It seemed that the priority was a large mug of coffee. Sitting with my hands around the comforting warmth of the mug, I stared through the large patio door and gazed at the garden. The glowing golden autumn had turned overnight into a dull, drizzling grey scene. I thought of John and wondered how he would be able to focus on a responsible job after all that he had gone through. Not for him the luxury of a comforting drink whenever he chose. For a rare time, I was so grateful to be a "mum at home." I appreciated being able to arrange my day as I chose and tackle the jobs as and when I felt able. I needed thinking time.

I was tired but my mind was clear, and as I sat and contemplated, it wandered backwards and forwards from weekend memories to future hopes and plans. I had four small practical overnight bags to unpack and some washing to do, but at the same time, there were the four unseen boxes of problems to open and the big question of which one to open first. One decision was easy. The box containing Charlie's spinal surgery was one I could not open. We were on a waiting list to see the consultant and the timing of this was out of our hands and easily left in God's hands. The box containing John's job change was out of my hands. All I could do was to scour the Thursday evening paper and report to John anything that looked hopeful but most of that box was his to unpack. I took the lid off the box containing the rebuilding of our marriage. I knew that it was not something we could do overnight. A long job lay ahead of us. It was to be a whole new learning experience and in our everyday lives our number one priority, for our sakes and that of the boys. I had already recognized that much of our difficulties had arisen through lack of honest communication, and all I could pull out of that box was the determined intention to be very honest and to give priority to spending more quality time with John. Babysitters had to be found and, as precious and important as Charlie and Sam were, they had to take second place. For their sakes, our marriage repair had to come first. On looking back, I have often wondered why God had allowed Charlie to have to face long and painful surgery when God was, as He had proved, well able to heal Charlie by just saying the word. Maybe, it was because in having to work through something so painful for parents as this, John and I were forced to work and pull together in a way we had never had to before. As we had to comfort Charlie and maintain security for Sam, we had to communicate well and stick close to each other.

The fourth box was the one I had to unpack and take responsibility for; the box containing my health. Yes, I was sane and had a clear mind but, for reasons I was not to understand for years to come, God had begun a healing but had sent me home in ever-increasing pain and accumulating other unpleasant symptoms that were so far unexplained. Here was an issue I could do something about by praying and trying to get the right medical help. God can and does perform miracles, but I do believe that healing takes time and He does use doctors in the process as He chooses to involve us simple humans in His plan, taking the talents, skills, and abilities He has given us. The tragic illness of AIDS was not known of at that time or I would have been far more worried than I was, but I did have to face what was to me unthinkable. Could John be a carrier of a sexually transmitted disease that presented no symptoms in him but was showing itself in me? Why oh why was God asking me yet again to face situations that were beyond my ability to endure? Questioning God about this was of no value. I had to trust He knew what He was doing, but I did not like it and let Him know in no uncertain terms, for which I know He has forgiven me! There was only one way to find the answer to the question that I could not face and that was to seek medical help, but from where?

"Why such a fuss about such an everyday medical problem," you are probably asking yourselves, but twenty-five years ago, attitudes to this were very different from today and especially in my family. Sex was more or less an unmentionable subject, and certainly one I could have not discussed with my parents. Forgiveness for John would have been out of the question and I would have been told that I had made my bed and must lie in it. For the saving of our marriage, it was vital that as few people knew as possible. So, where could I go?

I asked God and He said nothing. I could have asked John to seek medical help, but I did not want to dump more heaps of guilt upon him. The obvious place to go was to my doctor, but he was a partner in my father's practice. I knew he would be kind and that I could be certain that he would keep my situation confidential, but everything would be written on my medical records for anyone to read and gossip and so this was not an option for me. For a doctor's daughter, I was totally uninformed about how and where to go for help in the case of any problems. It was always the case that I went to my father who would always sort it out. Now, though I had to find my way through with Jesus. Daddy was no longer God in my life.

The unthinkable option seemed my only one and one about which I had no knowledge. I was out of my depth in a world way out of my experience. I had to go to a clinic for sexually transmitted diseases, but where were they? Were they at hospitals? I had heard of V.D. clinics mentioned in whispers (V.D. standing for venereal diseases) but the name alone carried such a stigma. Why was God putting me through this? I think he was chipping away at my pride. The Bible says that pride comes before destruction and God loved me enough to see me suffer the breaking of my pride in order to save me from destruction. Everyone has some pride, but when pride was on offer in life, I seemed to have helped myself to buckets full of it and the losing and breaking of pride is so very painful.

God had begun the process when I was forced to tell our tale of woe to Jim. Now, God was taking me one more painful step further.

As I searched the telephone directory for where to go, I suddenly remembered that I had known of a private clinic that was run as a charity to help young people with such problems. This seemed the right course of action and it would involve confidentiality away from my father's practice. However, I was wrestling with my pride. "Won't go!" "Shan't go!" "Can't go." This was a place for the promiscuous, for prostitutes, for common people with no morals. This was my view but not God's. It was for the prostitutes, the adulterers, and the outcasts that Jesus came. He knew their stories and lives and it was to them that he offered forgiveness. It was the socially unaccepted to whom he gave love and value and whose broken lives He mended. He restored their self worth. Who was I to think of myself as so much more important and precious to Him than they were? I was a sinner just as they were. Who was I to judge? It was my pride that elevated me above them and it needed dealing with and this was one way certain of success.

Once again, I needed a plan to cope and it was simple. I would use my birthday present from Jim. It was a woollen soft green knitted matching hat and scarf ready for the walks to school on the freezing winter days that were approaching.

I decided that if I pulled the hat down low enough and wrapped the scarf around most of my face and neck, with only my eyes peeping out, I would be well disguised. I could sneak into the place without anyone recognizing me. Confident that the plan was a good one, I phoned and made an appointment then waited for the dreaded day. "Won't go." "Shan't go." "Can't go." were silenced by the pelvic pain saying, "Must go." "Must know."

The wait seemed for eternity but the bustle, fights, and fun with the boys helped to speed up the time and eventually the day circled on the calendar arrived. Unaware of my knocking knees and quaking sinking heart, Charlie, Sam, and I set off for school, armed with cheese sandwiches, apples, chocolate bars, and very necessary hat and scarf. The bus stop was outside the school and I only had time for a quick kiss goodbye before the bus came. I paid my fare and then arranged my disguise. It was hot in the bus and the scarf covering my nose and mouth made breathing in the hot air a struggle but better suffocate than be recognized.

The clinic was in a large old house. I am no expert in architecture, but it may have been Victorian or Georgian. The important thing about it was that it did not feel medical. The reception area was carpeted and the receptionist was not wearing a uniform but a welcoming accepting smile. She took down my details and then kindly guided me to a waiting room. I pulled the hat down lower and the scarf up higher and surveyed the scene. Chairs were arranged all round the room, with a long coffee table in the centre of them holding a selection of magazines. The room was not crowded and the few people waiting were all reading the magazines, and so I decided hat this must be the procedure and helped myself to one. Its title or subject was of no consequence. It was not for reading. It was for hiding behind. I wondered how many of those present were actually reading. Were they all hiding too? If so, we were all very successful as our faces were completely hidden.

Looking down at the grey, heavy-duty carpet I decided to play a game. I would imagine that I was in a dentist's waiting room. My imagination failed me so I stared at my feet and legs, thus avoiding anyone else. My denim jeans and strong shoes to withstand eight walks each day up and down to school would have told anyone present that I was a young mother. Thus, began a new game. I would look at everyone else's legs and try to guess their occupations. One pair of black, patent, leather, fashionable shoes and elegant tights – a secretary? One pair of old jeans and dirty white trainers – a student? One pair of black trousers and classical leather shoes – an accountant? Whatever our occupations, we were united by our similar problems. Before I could play my game for long, my name (to my horror) was announced to all and I was ushered in to a nurse, wearing a uniform, who took my details and then handed me over to a doctor. They were all compassionate and non-judgmental, and the difficult but necessary investigations were soon over. Boldly ticking the box on the form withholding permission to pass on details to my doctor, I again put on my disguise and escaped as soon as possible, clutching a form on which was written the date of my follow-up appointment for my test results. Would they be a relief or the beginning of another traumatic nightmare?

As the bus stopped outside the school just in time to collect Charlie and Sam for lunch, their beaming faces and waving paintings drew me back into a more familiar and comfortable environment and, once home, their cuddles comforted me. My feelings of guilt, contamination, and failure were loved away and for two weeks some form of normality could return. Meanwhile, John, who was unaware of "adventures," began to open his box containing "look for a job." We were so certain that God wanted us to move north that the lack of job opportunities was so frustrating. Also, we were being very unsuccessful in trying to find an understanding and supportive church so we clung to Chris for all we were worth. Almost every Friday became "pack to go north for the weekend" and Charlie and Sam began to look forward to meeting their old friends who had gone ahead of us. We were helped and advised and loved there plus given the strength to battle on in our wilderness here. It was also so encouraging to see Jesus continue to heal and deliver in their meetings. He had not just given us a taste and then cleared off to leave us to get on without him.

Chris could do nothing more about the content of his problem box containing his house sale. That was all that he had to do and all he could do was wait. That must have been quite worrying and a test of his trust in Jesus as he now had no job and four children to feed. We met regularly, but not for long. With a speed beyond all our expectations, suddenly his "For Sale" board was replaced by "Sold". He was delighted, but we were devastated. We were to be left here, our friend and source of constant comfort and support gone, all alone bewildered, frightened, and lonely. Chris's possessions were loaded into boxes and driven away. I wiped streams of tears as I performed my final act of love and gratitude to them, vacuuming their carpets through a lifeless empty house in readiness for its new occupants. Chris had always been puzzled as to why the house had not sold when he, and everyone else, had been sure that the move was what God wanted. Now, he had the answer to his questions. He had, of necessity, been required by God to stay for our sakes. Throughout all the traumatic previous weeks, we would not have got through without him. He held us together, encouraged us, and gave stability to us and the boys until we were safe to leave. God's timing was perfect and we had to trust that it would be the same for us.

Alone and friendless, I made my visit to the clinic for the test results. What horrors lay ahead? Would I have some treatment to further my healing? I had no idea what to expect. The news was a mixture of good and bad. There was no evidence of any serious disease, but they had detected an unidentifiable bacterium that was not necessarily to do with John. I was advised to take a two-week course of antibiotics. This was the bad news because, although they could provide contraception, they could not prescribe antibiotics and so I had to go to my doctor, the one thing I wanted to avoid. Clutching the paper containing the information for him, I sat on the bus questioning God. "Why!" The answer was clear. It was yet again a breaking of my pride. I was proud of being a good wife, of being a good mother, of having a successful marriage. Now, just as with Jim, the truth was to come out. I was a failure. I had made mistakes. I could no longer pretend to be Mrs Perfect and it hurt so much.

I waited until Charlie and Sam had gone to bed before telling John about the events of the previous weeks. I felt entirely right to have kept it from him until now. There was no need for him to suffer another heap of guilt dumped on him. We prayed and then phoned Dr Frank, my father's partner and good friend. Trying to keep my emotions under control, I asked if he would see us to discuss something that had arisen concerning my health and requested that he would not tell my father that we were consulting him, even though he knew how worried my father was and was well aware of my health situation. His response was just as I had expected, one of kindness, concern, and helpfulness. He even offered to visit our house so that we could avoid going to the surgery.

The following day, the three of us settled down with a cup of tea. Through tears and whimpering mixed with deep embarrassment, we blurted out our story. He listened with compassion as we made our way through the shame, the failure, our broken hearts, and our experiences. To try and rescue some of our shattered reputation, I told him that God had asked me to forgive and that I was making my way, if falteringly, through this. John's tears showed his repentance without any need for words. We told him that we were determined to save our marriage and of how we had re-married in the Cotswolds. We showed him our new wedding rings. He was so understanding, and it was not as difficult as I had expected to pour out our woe. He was the only person apart from my parents-in-law and our support team in the church who knew anything of all of this, and he cared for us. Handing me a prescription, he left us saying, "It was better here than at the surgery, wasn't it?" I knew I could count on his promise of confidentiality and I felt safe. He wished us well and offered further help if we needed it. As I stood in the porch to wave him goodbye, my eyes looked over the road to the woods opposite and to the entrance a little further down the road. It was then that it hit me like a bolt from heaven. The wedding dress dream had happened just as I had dreamt it. I remembered the dream so well because it was so unusual. In the dream, as you will remember too, I had walked across to the woods wearing a beautiful wedding dress and had handed an invitation to our wedding to Dr. Frank. Today, that had actually happened as we had invited him, the only person, into our private second marriage. I wonder why I dreamt it. If I had known when I woke after the dream all that would have happened, I do not think I could have faced it. However, now with the dream become reality, it had shown me that God knew what was to happen before I did. I was reassured that He is in full control of our futures and is working for our good. When times are hard, it is a strength to remember this. I do not expect all my dreams to be signs of the future ahead, but there are a few that I hold in my heart and wait to see what will happen. The longer I live through this life, the more God has proved to me that what He has said is true. The dream, together with other experiences, convinces me of the truth of God's words in Jeremiah 29:11.

"I know the plans I have for you," declares the Lord, "Plans to prosper you and not to harm you, plans to give you hope and a future."

Chapter 13

Purpose

On and on, minute by minute, day by day, month after month, the pain increasingly tormented me. A short walk now resulted in sharp pains in my knees and shooting pains down my sciatic nerve at the back of my legs. I was having to face the fact that walking the boys to school was becoming more difficult, and at some time, I was going to have to trust God to protect them as, without other mothers walking that way, they would have to hold hands and go alone. To distract me from this problem, burning skewers of pain drilled through my eyeballs and where I once wore my hat disguise I now wore a constant migraine type headache. With no medication and no whisky, I had to find my way through with Jesus, but what could He do?

I found a way of comforting my pelvic pain by kneeling with my tummy against the bedroom radiator and my arms crossed on the window ledge. The warmth relaxed and helped a little. Tonight, however, I had had enough. I collapsed to my knees and pressed against the radiator, and with my arms on the window ledge rested my head on my arms. From this warm position, I observed the night-time scene through our bedroom window. We were high up and I could see the rooftops of hundreds of houses. Tiny lights shone brightly in their upstairs windows against a backdrop of a velvety dark navy blue sky. People were going to bed. I considered how small each person would be. How tiny each precious one is in this enormous world in which my whole view was only a speck. I thought how enormous God must be and how amazing beyond understanding that He knew everything about everyone. As I thought, I threw out of the window a despairing cry. "How, Jesus, did you stand the pain?" It was not a prayer but a cry. It seems incredible, but our incredible God heard my plaintive despair. As I gazed into the darkness of that velvet night sky, I actually saw on it a golden cross and a soft voice said, "Look beyond the cross."

For days, and often through the years, I have meditated on those words and it would fill many books to put down all the strengthening thoughts and encouragement I have taken from them. Our lives are so short in terms of eternity and our pain in this life not to be compared with the promise of the bliss to come. To focus beyond the pain and into the vastness of eternity would be my way through. To aim for what is yet to come would overcome pain. Jesus had the personal knowledge of where He had left to come to earth and also to where he was returning. I could only imagine the unimaginable and dream the certain promise of no more pain, crying, weeping, or mourning given to us by our God who is making all things new. A new world to come.

My cry was followed by a whining moan. I have a worrying feeling that Charlie inherits his whining from me!

"But I'm just not enjoying life," I complained, then listened attentively as the soft understanding voice continued to say,

"I did not come to enjoy life but to accomplish the purpose for which my Father sent me. If you are to follow me, it will be the same for you."

That was to be the only time I can say that I believe God actually spoke to me. Life would be so easy if he would always tell us what to do and boom instructions from Heaven. As His words floated over the rooftops, I thought of all I knew of Jesus. He went to weddings and I am sure he enjoyed them. He had friends whose company he enjoyed. He liked a glass of wine and I am sure he enjoyed that. He could not have been a moaning misery for people to have been drawn towards him and fascinated by him. However, he was called also a man of sorrows. He cried with grief. He endured misunderstanding, mocking, flogging rejection, and pain. Yes, He did not come for his own enjoyment, but for us. He came to show the love of God and to heal us. Whether at a wedding or a party or suffering abuse and agony, he was firmly fixed on his purpose and aim, the cross.

He came to die so that through faith in him our relationship with God, our father, could be healed and we could know his forgiveness and his passionate love. If it was to be the same for me, I had to find my unique purpose in life in order to find my way through. I needed a fixed attitude and obedience to overcome my pain and produce something of value out of it. Knowing Jesus' passionate love for me I wanted to be able, one day, to give him something back, a little thank you from me.

It took me at least a year to find out what my specific purpose was. I listened to people, I observed my own behaviour. I looked back at the lives of my ancestors for four generations and watched Charlie and Sam. I am forever indebted to a wonderful teacher of Bible application called Derek Prince whose tapes helped me so much in my search.

I studied child psychology and learnt all I could about marriage. It sounds a lot to do but I had to do it in order to survive. I especially looked at Jesus's cross, finding out that it was far more than an execution.

When Jesus died, he turned bad for good for those who would believe and follow him. However, we cannot just say "He did it." We have to work it out in our own individual lives. He changed all our worst shameful deeds into forgiveness, our rejection into acceptance, our filth into cleanliness. Our sicknesses he turned into healing, our poverty into riches, our despair into hope, and our death into eternal life. He turned curse into blessing.

Partly because of occult activity in the lives of my ancestors and compounded by my own failure, I concluded that this was to be my purpose for my life. I was to work with Jesus in order to set Charlie and Sam and the generations to come free from the curse of the past. This was to be the goal on which I had to fix my eyes.

It was to cost me every waking moment. There was to be no career for me. I had to learn, correcting wrong beliefs and behaviour, and then pass it on. I had to free the boys from all control, domination, and manipulation so that they could discover who they really were, not what I wanted them to be. They needed to be released into freedom with responsibility. All criticism had to be replaced with praise, lies with truth. All superstition had to be banished. They needed unconditional love with loads of hugs and smiles and approval. It was vital that they felt accepted, however they went wrong. I am so grateful that God gave me John as their father. He was so different from me, and his upbringing, though not perfect, brought balance into the harshness of my young life. His input was vital and as I submitted to him a better future lay ahead for our sons. It was to be such a difficult purpose to fulfil, and at times so frightening, but the fear that ruled my life had to be broken in this life just as it had been on the cross.

"Burrr!" "Yeah!" "Burrr!" "Burrr!" "Yeah!" "Ouch! That hurt." "Burrr!" "Ow!"

"Burrr!" "Tell him Mum." "Ow." "Stop him Mum!" "Burrr!"

It was becoming obvious that Easter Chicken and Scotty Bear were beginning a fight to the death. It quickly led me to the conclusion that bedtime was to be half an hour early tonight. Firmly grasping one small wrist in each hand, they were marched up the stairs to the bathroom where the washing of faces and the cleaning of teeth began to calm the atmosphere. Soon, warmly tucked up side by side in their little twin beds, the bedtime routine began. Little heads were stroked and a bedtime song sung softly. (Perhaps that is why neither of them grew up to follow me into a career in music!) Stories of Tibs, Tabs, and Timothy were told then, having said their prayers, they were kissed "Goodnight" and the bedroom door gently shut.

That, however, was never the end of it because now came my favourite part. I could sit on the stair outside the bedroom and listen to their childish conversation as they dropped off to sleep. Nosy, was not I? It was useful though, as I learnt much about them as they shared their thoughts with each other. Tonight was about to be a treat for me. They were to discuss the miraculous power of Jesus.

"Ch-ch Charlie," stuttered Sam in his high squeaky voice

"Yes," replied Charlie, about to give his full attention

"You know … you know, when Jesus fed all … all them lots of people with just them … them loaves and fishes. H..how did he do it? Was it magic?"

"Don't be stupid, Sam," answered Charlie with assurance and wisdom.

"He cut them into soldiers."

For those of you for whom the term " soldiers" is unfamiliar, it is the term we use in the Midlands for cutting up bread and butter to eat dipped in a runny boiled egg!

How wonderful and trusting children are. For them it is so simple, no complex debates, no religious arguments. They can go to sleep in peace, and they did.

FEAR, FEAR, FEAR. Another enemy had come to torment me. All my life I had been an anxious person, but this was much bigger. It was fear. It began my day and accompanied me through my day until sleep came. Initially, having the boys to care for helped me to overcome it, but with each new day, its intensity increased. I tried to work out what it was that I feared. Was it the pain? Was it the illness? Was it reaction to all that we had been through? I certainly was concerned about the uncertainty of our future, but the concern did not warrant fear as great as this.

I managed in the weekdays, but at the weekends, with John to help with Charlie and Sam, it changed from fear to terror. After a night's sleep, as I surfaced to face a new day, the fear hit me before the awareness of pain. It became paralysing. Eventually, I was finding it impossible to get out of bed. Our experiences had convinced us that Jesus could take it away, but what should we do?

We called the folks in the fellowship and they were praying for us, but the situation was not improving and I was really struggling. I should have learnt by now that it is when we are at our wits end that God takes over.

I hung over the edge of the bed and through my terror reached for the red telephone hanging on the wall. In desperation, I rang Robert's number that I keep in my head for spiritual emergencies. To hear that soft Scottish accent merely saying his name brought comfort and reassurance.

Just the sound of his voice said "All will be well." With teeth chattering, I stuttered out my terror.

"I don't know what to do," was not the answer I was counting on.

"We had better pray."

Before I could think, this lovely kind voice started praying in his own special language that God had given him. I had not a clue what he was saying, and nor had he, but God knew and it felt warming. Funny to think that somewhere in the world this could be an everyday language for someone and they would understand every word. Funny too to think that somewhere across the world some small person might be crying out to God in English, not understanding their prayers but speaking out in faith and trust.

As Robert finished his prayer, he said, "I have a feeling that God is going to do something for you in the night. I don't know what it is but don't try to work it out, just accept it."

I was baffled. Robert sounded so confident and I was so terrified. I went to bed that night wondering what on earth (or in Heaven) would happen. I was almost afraid to go to sleep, but I should have rested knowing that God never harms us.

As I slept I dreamt. I could see my Christian Grandma and my Grandpa standing behind a kitchen table. Grandma was smiling and cuddly as always. When I looked at Grandpa's face, he wore the kindest loving soft smile, and his eyes sparkled.

"I thought he was dead." I said to my Grandma, mystified (my grandpa had died when I was two.)

"No, he's alive." she replied smiling happily, and as they turned towards one another I woke up.

Over breakfast, I reported what had happened to John and he, in his usual practical way, said "Well you had better do what Robert told you to and accept it."

"What did it have to do with the fear?" I wondered. I was not afraid all day because my grandpa had died. The strange thing about the dream was that his expression was so soft and I remembered him through my childish eyes as stern and ferocious. However, at the least it was a lovely thought that he was alive in eternity and I would one day see him again.

"The bungalow! The bungalow!" squeaked Sam as he climbed into his seat in the back of the car. Visiting my mother was always a happy time for the boys, and they eagerly anticipated the treats and spoiling that lay ahead for them. Whilst they sat on the floor drawing over the carpet pattern with their fingers, John and I nestled on the sofa with a cup of tea.

"What was Pam's grandpa like?" queried John.

"Oh, he was the softest kindest person and he loved Pam so much. He always called her his sunshine," answered my mother, adding "We could never understand why Pam was so terrified of him."

Terror no more. Fear no more. Now, I am looking forward in our next life to meeting him again and throwing my arms around the man whose mouth was identical to that of my father and telling him that I love him. The lie I had believed about him for so long was gone forever and I knew we had eternity in which to share our love for each other.

Chapter 14

⌢

Searching New Depths

We wondered and we puzzled, moaned, and complained.

"Why no job, why was I still so ill, why were we alone?"

We took comfort from Chris's delay and knew we had to trust that there was a good reason that one day we would understand. Never before had we been so grateful for the invention of the telephone. At least, we could contact our friends for comfort and advice. They were equally confused. They had seen such enormous miracles in our lives so why the hold up?

God had chosen to leave my healing incomplete so why? We learnt that there can be blocks in someone's life that God wants to clear, but in my case what were they? Unforgiveness is a big one that lets in bitterness. I had forgiven everyone who had hurt me to the best of my ability. Unbelief was another but having gone through so much, if I did not believe, then I certainly did now. Unconfessed sin was another, and I had confessed all I could think of. Unconfessed sin on John's part could be a factor and just the thought made me shudder, but he too had revealed all. Unexpectedly, an elder of the fellowship was praying about all this and all he could think of was "water," but what could that have to do with this. He asked us and we were completely unable to throw any light on it, but then light came to him.

"Have you been baptized?" he asked, continuing to briefly explain that baptism opens the way to further deeper spiritual experiences. John and I were Christened as babies, as were Charlie and Sam. I thought of this as a sort of heavenly insurance policy for them. The baptism Jesus received was by being fully immersed in water. We had heard of it in Baptist churches, but never given it a thought. The fellowship was not "churchy" and we did not realize that they were mostly all baptized. We were given some books and tapes to explain it all, but yet again, it was all beyond me. For me, it was simple. If Jesus did it, he was showing an example for us to follow. I had chosen to follow him so it was "Into the water she goes!" John made the same choice and we asked Colin if he would baptize us at the fellowship and he agreed.

I was taken aback by everyone's reaction to this. Anyone would have thought we had won the Lottery. People became mega-excited and started planning as if it was a party, or as if we had suddenly become royalty. All became clearer as they told their own experiences after baptism. It was obviously "big".

"The mighty power of God just fell on me."

"I was instantly healed of my back problem."

"I felt ecstatic."

"I felt so near to God."

"I felt so clean."

The more I heard the more hopeful and excited I became myself. I think John probably applied his, "Let's judge it at the end."

I became quite nervous a few days before we went. We had explained to the boys, who were getting even more used to the three-hour journey, and Charlie was interested in the prospect of Dad and Mum getting wet. Double the amount of packing this time. One case for dry and one for wet! My imagination went wilder as the day drew near. Would God heal me? This question was followed in my mind by the awful thought.

"Could I be in this not for love of Jesus but to get the healing that I wanted?" I decided to ignore this thought.

Looking over the banisters, I observed a small grey animal, soon to be identified as Sam, half covered in his duffel coat packing his essentials into his blue plastic case. The blue case accompanied him everywhere and he usually wore a sailor hat at the same time. Its vital contents were the hat, Easter Chicken, four felt tip pens, a colouring book, and a corner of a sheet. Just what everyone wants for an occasion so spiritually significant!

Into the car and off again. Being early November, it was dark and the journey seemed long but audio tape stories lulled the boys to sleep. Normally, that would have been a disaster heralding a night awake, but the baptism was to be that evening and we needed them awake.

The fellowship had nowhere that held enough water to "dunk" one adult let alone two, so they took us to a local church. It was made of old grey stone and had pillars and an open courtyard. My goodness, it was cold that night. The wind was bitter and howled through the courtyard and we were given a small vestry with a tiny inefficient electric fire beside which we could change. Freeze to death! A small price to pay to be healed!

Suitably dressed in dark clothes to avoid revealing all once wet, I held John's hand as we entered the baptism room. It was slightly warmer in there, probably because of all the people gathered around the water. It was like a mini swimming pool with small waterproof tiles around the edge. Charlie was sitting on the tiles dangerously near the edge, but that caused me no concern as he rarely moved and was very obedient. A greater concern was Sam sitting next to him, happily colouring a racing car green. My worries fled as I could see Chris hanging on to the back of Sam's trousers.

In the water, Colin was already up to his knees. I was not prepared for the moment to come as we were both asked to confess our faith and give a small talk about what had led us to this point. I left most of this to John who was well used to addressing people in his work and I just mumbled some agreement, then, tentatively dipping a toe in to test the temperature, hand in hand John and I joined Colin in the water. I had no idea really what to expect, but as Colin put his hand on my shoulder, it became clear I was to be first.

"Upon confession of your faith in Jesus Christ," sounded Colin's dignified and educated voice " baptize you in".......

"My green's run out!" shrieked and squealed in my left ear, and then all I saw was bubbles until I was pulled out of the water and standing wiping my eyes.

What did I feel? Where was the mighty power of God? Where was that feeling of closeness? Was I healed? I knew exactly what I felt. I felt wet. I felt very wet and freezing! I watched John's baptism whilst shivering and dithering all over and as we crossed the open courtyard, I think I was the most cold I have ever been in my life. Huddled by the electric fire, we compared our experiences. I had never been so disappointed and the misery took days to come to terms with. I knew God loved me. I had no doubt. He had not healed me. It was all the same and nothing had changed.

It is only after many years that I have more understanding of the significance of baptism in the spiritual world and the spiritual war in which we are fighting. If we had not been baptized, the future for us and particularly for Charlie and Sam would have been very different. Let us judge it at the end!

Chapter 15

A Box Opens

November was filled with the smell of baking mince pies and Christmas cake, with glue and paper, shopping trips, and bouncing boys. We made our annual trip to the forest to choose the Christmas tree and have the usual arguments. "That one's too tall." "That one's leaning." The chosen blue, green spruce with little cones on it was taken home to the garage to be dried via a stop for beef-burger buns. I love Christmas. It was even more special for us now as we brought the olive wood stable down from the loft and retold the story of Jesus' birth as we put the lambs and shepherds in their place. Our little gifts were placed under the tree. Charlie and Sam were very excited, but John and I were only too aware that, also under the tree were our problem boxes. What would the baby in the manger do about them? We knew that he had already opened them and dealt with them two thousand years before, but how would he want us to work through this in our lives with Him?

Almost as soon as the Christmas washing up was done, a problem box opened much sooner than expected. We knew it contained Charlie's spinal surgery, but it contained extras that were unexpected. In today's shopping terms, it would be "Buy one get one free!" As if one problem was not enough, there was a second and it belonged to John. It was to be a real test of his commitment to Jesus and to us, and to this day I do not know how difficult it was for him.

John had a difficult and very responsible job. It had been one of his gods and he took great pride in it. For several months he had been involved in an ongoing project, which was drawing to a very satisfactory end. There was to be a conclusion to be held in Portugal and all the most important members of the team were to be there. There would be feasts, speeches, champagne, and celebration. This was to be John's moment of glory, well deserved for so much hard work, and he so much was looking forward to it. I did not want him to go. It was not that I felt jealous, but I really needed him to help with the boys as my health made caring for them such a struggle.

An unrecognized and unexpected envelope came through the letter box that day. All day I wondered what it contained. It did not look like a bill but it looked sort of important. After the boys' bedtime, we read the post and opened the mysterious envelope. There was the appointment for Charlie to see the orthopaedic consultant and the prospective date for his operation. Of course, you will have guessed. The date was right in the middle of the Portugal conference.

"The consultant will change it," John said, waving the letter around with confidence, but that was not to be. The hospital could not take Charlie any earlier and the consultant was about to retire and the date we had been given was the only one. John now had to choose. Would he stay with his son in his time of pain or would he go for the glory?

For the old John, there would have been no question. He would be packing his case already, but he was not the old John but a new one. He had a few weeks in which to decide.

I had to watch him agonize and myself resist the temptation to go back to my old ways and manipulate him.

With the promise of a currant bun and a cup of coffee in the supermarket restaurant opposite later, John and I, holding Charlie between us, climbed the old stone steps of the children's hospital. I hate hospitals and having left the neurosurgical hospital vowed that I would never enter one again. How wrong could I have been! I had my own appointments, then Charlie's adenoids, Charlie's ears, Charlie's toes, and what was to come would be the hardest for us all. Charlie was his normal calm, smiling self. He knew exactly why he was there and was by now well used to a hospital atmosphere.

We counted twenty stone steps and twenty searing pains shot down my legs. I had no idea how I would physically cope with at least three weeks of this. "Oh please God tell John to stay."

The hospital was ancient with green tiled corridors that seemed to go on endlessly. It would have been gloomy in the extreme, except it was obvious that there were some people who were doing their best to make it cheerful for the children. Brightly colourful cartoons stood out on the tiles and mobiles hung from the ceilings. We later learnt that all this was done voluntarily by a team called, "Radio Lollipop," who also broadcast music and messages into the wards for the children. All the staff were smiling and laughing and we knew we were in a happy and cheering place.

With little waiting, Charlie was called into the consulting room and the three of us faced Mr Dorritt, "the man for the job." He was elderly but kind and well used to talking to children. He made Charlie feel important (with which Charlie would agree). He showed Charlie, then us, his X rays and proceeded to explain the plan. He would remove one of Charlie's ribs and make it into a sort of polyfilla.

He would then remove a triangle of bone in his spine that should not be there and inactivate the growing plates on one side of each vertebra so that the curve would correct as Charlie grew. He would then polyfilla the bones together in a spinal fusion. It would be an eight-hour operation, then three weeks in hospital, and one year in plaster.

John asked whether the date could be altered, but there was no choice. It was then or never. Mr Dorritt was the expert in the country for this type of surgery and our choice was "yes" or "no," with John or without him. John and I had known that the operation had serious risks, paralysis being only one, but if we chose against the surgery, Charlie would be fine until his teenage growing spurt then he would keel over sideways and have breathing problems as his left lung became more and more compressed. We had agreed the surgery, but why so much pain for Charlie? God could heal him, why did he allow a child to suffer?

I still firmly believed that there was time for God to intervene and I was not going to give up asking him until as long as it took. Charlie was quite placid about the whole experience. If it had been Sam in his place, the whole of the West Midlands would be hearing about it!

At this point, John became "brave" and explained our experience of God lengthening Charlie's leg. Risking being labelled "mad," he told Mr Dorritt the full story and requested that Charlie should be re X-rayed. Mr Dorritt showed no emotion at this bizarre request and to our amazement agreed. He then wrote on Charlie's notes "Parents are Christian but sensible about it" (words we smile about regularly)

The result of the new X-rays showed a slight change in Charlie's pelvic tilt, but the necessity for surgery was obvious unless there was a miracle to come. The date was set and we set off for our currant buns and a difficult decision for John.

PORTUGAL "To go or not to go. That was the question." John prayed a lot and asked the advice of others. My father instantly said, "Go to Portugal," and so did many work colleagues. When the men at the fellowship were asked, they said they would pray but never gave their opinion as the choice had to be made by John. He agonized and I knew how torn he must have felt. To lose the praise after all the work. It was a once-in-a-lifetime opportunity.

It became decision time and John sat with his head in his hands covering his eyes. What was I to expect? I knew what John wanted for himself and I knew my father's opinion held a lot of weight for John.

"I'm staying with Charlie. I can't leave him."

These words came from a new John, the father I wanted for our sons and the husband I needed. Through tears I thanked him and we prepared for the big day.

Everything was well explained to Charlie and he knew to expect pain, but he was his usual placid smiling self when he looked back towards his home from the car. As we passed his school, he gave it a wave. The steps to the hospital were familiar now but not the long ward, cheerfully decorated by the volunteers. Charlie was shown his bed and most impressed by the square piece of sheepskin at the end of it.

"That's nice and soft," he commented whilst running his fingers through the wool. Feeling such luxury, he began to behave as if he was on holiday in a four-star hotel. Charlie was a friendly little chap and was soon moving from bed to bed chatting to the other children. So many were so ill, some being there for their tenth operation in their short lives. They were so brave and accepting. I felt ashamed of my own weakness and moaning.

Undressed and lying with his tummy on the bed and feeling the sheepskin with his feet, Charlie enjoyed having his back shaved and then he and I were shown into another room with an enormous ancient metal bath in it. Into the warm water he leapt, splashing around happily as I rubbed his misshapen back with a sponge. I was not at all happy. Here was my healthy son, free from pain and possibly facing a disaster, and I was responsible together with John for our decision. Charlie had had no choice. He was too young to make such a choice. As I stroked his golden hair and looked at his back I thought,

"You have no idea. Tomorrow they are going to cut your back open, break your spine and you may never walk again."

"You could heal him tonight, 'I cried to God.' You could spare him."

I had to trust God in this, but I still believed for a last minute miracle for Charlie. Walking back to bed with Charlie wrapped in a towel, my heart leapt as I could see a miracle about to happen. There, by his bed, were friends from the fellowship who had travelled for over four hours to come and pray for him. "What faith and commitment," I thought as their warm hugs comforted me. They prayed and then departed as suddenly as they had arrived, leaving us to tuck Charlie up in bed.

God knew Charlie better than we did and He had a treat in store for him. Radio Lollipop was broadcasting into the ward and they welcomed him by name and played him a song, but even greater treat than that, they were to hold a nightly competition. Charlie was passionate about competitions and as soon as he heard the word it was all we could do to keep him in bed. Not only did he join in but he won! Waving his £1 voucher prize in delight, he had already decided that this was to be a good experience. John's decision was proved to be so necessary as we had not realized that a parent was needed twenty-four hours a day after surgery and with Sam to care for, I could not have done it alone.

With a serious expression, Mr Dorritt strode up the ward, his eyes fixed on Charlie.

"Are you comfortable, young man?" he asked kindly whilst checking his notes. "I will see you in the operating theatre tomorrow."

"God could heal him tonight." My words were quiet and weak, trying to find some faith but feeling it drizzling away.

"God or no God, I shall see you in the operating theatre tomorrow," Mr Dorritt declared in a loud authoritative voice that attempted to crush all my hope.

Prayers said and tucked up, the placid Charlie was happy to kiss us goodbye and see us tomorrow, but would he see Mr Dorritt in the operating theatre?

We arrived in plenty of time, but God is greater than any man. I have learnt after many years that to declare the future and raise our plans above God's plans is a recipe for disaster. Pride comes before destruction. Mr Dorritt did not see Charlie in the operating theatre. It was not Charlie's back alone that God was dealing with, but a far wider plan involving His work in all our lives. Charlie was not healed in the night but Mr Dorritt was struck down. He developed gout in his elbow overnight and was unable to work. I often wonder if he remembered his strong words as he lay awake in pain escheduling his theatre list. To have prepared ourselves for that day only to be postponed left John and me feeling like deflated balloons. Charlie, however, waving his £1 voucher was happily heading for a currant bun and a spending spree!

The following week seemed like eternity then suddenly we were back at the hospital for an action replay. This time it was the real thing and Mr Dorritt was more cautious in his words. Charlie was wheeled away for theatre early and we had eight hours to fill. What do

Christians who are sensible do at such times? I am sure all Christians reading this would answer "fast and pray" and that is, I am certain, the sensible approach. Our way through was different. We bought a bottle of red wine and went to bed! I learnt later that my father had shut himself in his study all day and refused to come out. He loved Charlie (his little mate) so much and with his medical knowledge of possible complications, it must have been so hard for him.

Eight hours later, we were sitting on two chairs beside an empty place waiting for Charlie's bed to arrive. "I wonder if he's with the little boy whose Daddy's a carpenter," I thought. Rather, like a police escort for royalty, a nurse walked in front of Charlie's bed as it was wheeled in, drips hanging from metal poles and followed by a significant number of medical staff. The drips went into a limp hand under an immaculate sheet, and golden hair rested on the white pillow. At the end of the bed, the sheet was folded back exposing two pink feet.

"Can you move your feet, Charlie?" asked a doctor.

The feet stayed limp and immobile.

"Try to move your feet, Charlie," encouraged a couple of nurses. There was no response.

"Can you hear them, Charlie?" I tried, "Move your feet."

Still no response. By this time everyone was holding their breath and looking anxiously at each other. Time stood still.

"Wigle your toes, Charlie," a young doctor whispered into Charlie's ear. Two pink feet moved up and down and everyone breathed out sighs of relief. Charlie was not paralysed. "Oh thank you, Jesus."

For Charlie, the moving of his feet was not a serious issue. He had more important things on his mind as he surfaced from the anaesthetic. His head rolling towards John, he opened his eyes and then closed them again.

"Have we missed the competition, Dad?" a faint voice asked. It was then that we knew Charlie was fine.

The three weeks ahead, we all remember as a happy time. Charlie's attitude helped so much and we became closer as a family as we pulled together. John took the night shifts entitling him to a cooked breakfast and daily competitions. Charlie gathered more vouchers and lots of cards. For the first week, Sam went to stay with his grandparents and daily we saw God moving a step ahead of us as all our needs were provided. Sam's teacher happened to live behind Grandpa's bungalow and so she took Sam in the car to school. I took over the day shift and raced back to collect Sam after school and take him to visit Charlie.

Charlie was not allowed to sit up, but he could lie on his side. Each time he saw Sam's small duffel-coated figure striding up the ward carrying his blue case, his eyes lit up and his smile brought tears to our eyes. Sam always took something special for him in the case, a drawing from school, a car, or a half-eaten pack of polo mints. We made fun amidst the pain, and I realized that God was mending our marriage as we grew closer through the experience we shared with the boys.

Charlie taught me a lot about attitude in those days. One day, he had to be taken by ambulance to another hospital to be plastered. With his teddy tucked under his arm, his bed was wheeled across the open car park to the ambulance. "Why today of all days did it rain?" I questioned.

"Move him quickly," a nurse instructed the porter urgently.

"No, slow down," begged Charlie. "The rain's lovely on my face and the fresh air's so nice."

The teddy was plastered first, then Charlie, and one week later they returned home to make a wonderful recovery.

We now had some idea why we had not been able to move north. Here, we had one of the top surgeons for Charlie's problem, friends were near, family supported, and every need was met.

One problem box was now empty and maybe we could open another and find a church until we moved.

Chapter 16

Goodbye

All the busyness during the time Charlie's back was healing did nothing to distract me from the ever-increasing pain and disability. Medically, there was no explanation and no hope. We knew our hope lay in Jesus. It was encouraging to hear from our fellowship friends of the wonderful things God was doing there and of their deepening friendships and relationships. At the same time, it was so frustrating. Job opportunities were few, and the ones that John applied for and would have done well seemed always to be closed doors.

So alone we sat and begged, "Please Jesus give us people who would understand our situation and support us until you can move us."

The only person we found was a Christian colleague at John's company. He understood, but we had lived through experiences that were beyond his own. He prayed with John and his church did the little they could and sent kind gifts of Lego to Charlie. All we could do was wait, suffer, and make the best of it.

"Hurray, hurray, hurray! It's tea at Grandpa's today!"

As the car pulled up outside the bungalow door, Charlie and Sam had already released themselves from their car seats and were attempting to get out of the back doors in a rush to ring the doorbell. Although plastered now, Charlie was growing taller and the bell, now in reach, rang continuously until answered. Grandpa bent down and threw one arm around each of the boys and hugged them. He used to scoop them up but they were getting too heavy now. They raced past the familiar copper bowl of flowers in the hall and to where my mother was sitting in her favourite chair, knitting and drinking tea. For most knitters it was knit one, purl one, but for her it was knit one purl one, sip one! On this particular day, she was painstakingly knitting tiny fine stitches of bottle green wool into small matching Guernsey sweaters for the boys. Anyone owning a Guernsey sweater would appreciate what a long and time-consuming occupation she undertook. Each stitch was knitted with love, and I wish today, I had been more appreciative of the love she showed in this way. That pain gets in the way of gratitude is no excuse.

Beside the chair was the wooden framed bag in which she kept her knitting needles and wool. If asked to estimate the cost of the contents of the bag, she probably would have said approximately thirty pounds. Little did she or any of us know that today it contained a treasure of unknown value. The room had become unusually quiet as the boys had eagerly followed Grandpa into the kitchen to help make sandwiches. We could hear the three of them rioting in the distance. Taking another sip of tea, mother reached down into the wool bag and produced something small and rectangular in her hand.

"I was given this and thought it might interest you," she said, passing me a plastic case containing an audiotape. I wonder what she would think of DVDs today. I was so unlike my mother in every way except that we shared a love of music, and I am forever grateful for her encouragement towards me in that. Many times she took me as a teenager to prom concerts or to join in the orchestra accompanying her operatic society. What so far unheard symphony had she found for me today? Looking at the back of the cassette, it was a collection of songs, but it was their titles that amazed me. They were all about our spiritual war and worship of Jesus.

"These people sound like your new friends" she commented casually, still not having grasped the enormity of what had happened to us.

"Where on earth did you get this from?" we asked, perplexed.

"It came from your father's cousin, Greg. He wrote the songs and has started a group of people like yours who meet in a scout hut."

We turned the cassette over and read the details. I am not sure if I had ever met Greg before in my life as he was part of a large collection of relations with whom I had little contact. It was enough for us to think that these people would understand us, and as they were only a twenty minute drive from our home, they might be able to help. We gave my mother a kiss and placed the tape in my pocket intending to call Greg as soon as possible. It was such a small action to hand over a piece of plastic. Could a cassette tape help us on our way north? God does always move in unexpected ways. I think it must be so that we can know that it is him at work in our lives and we cannot do anything for ourselves. He gets the praise and all we can do is obey. I am certain that as my mother gave us the tape, she did not bow down low and say, "Lord, it is my privilege to obediently hand over this instrument for their guidance," but God was using her for the outworking of his plan for us and one day I hope to see her receive her reward.

For the boys, it was to be an early bedtime that night. They were exhausted from their excitement and we were eager to call Greg. Having explained that we were related and we had been given a copy of his music, he began to talk with enthusiasm about his fellowship and his personal relationship with Jesus. He knew exactly what we were talking about. He never pushed his beliefs on us or tried to "Grab us for God," but in a friendly black country accent offered us any help he could give. Armed with directions to the scout hut, we said our goodbyes and waited for the weekend so that we could see what they were up to!

If a scout hut could bulge and jump, this one would have done so. We could hear the noise before we stepped out of the car. It was a sound of happy people, tuning of guitars, and general bustle. Inside, we found babies and toddlers everywhere and welcoming smiles and laughter. Charlie and Sam quickly were swept into the racing of toy cars and hurling of teddies as mothers did their best to gather their families together at the same time as bottle feeding twins. It seemed chaotic.

As Greg's band finished tuning up and began to play a recognizable tune, families appeared to automatically migrate to their chairs and we sat to observe the morning. It was a strange experience. I had always wondered why Charlie looked so unlike John and me and from where did his golden hair come? Seeing Greg singing and playing his guitar, it was just like looking at a large Charlie. Charlie could have been his son. So it was from my father's side of the family that Charlie inherited his looks. The songs were different from those we knew so well up north, but the words told the same story. As the louder songs of joy turned to gentle songs of love for Jesus, they touched my heart and the small voice I had heard by my bedroom window said,

"Say goodbye to your friends who have left. You have come home."

I was devastated. I cried my eyes out. My heart was set on moving. It was to be our new start in a new place. We were to see miracles there. I was to be healed there. I did not want to stay here. Our friends were all there. I did not want to stay with strangers. I was utterly heartbroken. As everything we had gone through was so new to us and so overwhelming, I had been going on my feelings. I had in my mind thought that Jesus had packed his bags and moved north. Now, I had to trust that he was everywhere and was just as powerful here as anywhere else in the world. I had to put my security in him and not people. I had to have faith that he would be here for us. It would have been so hard except that we had a "gut instinct" respect for the new fellowship leader who was expecting miracles himself with confidence. He was preaching the truth and everyone was so friendly, hospitable, and kind.

Would Jesus be in that place? Would he answer our prayers? In my distress I totally missed the fact that the very reason we were there was the answer to our prayers for people who would understand our experience and give us support. They not only gave us support but their very lives commitment to us, sharing all they had and were. I am forever grateful to all of them and as I observe Charlie and Sam as adult men, I know I could not have brought them up as they are without the love and care of these people. Thank you all. You gave them what I could not give. You are so special.

We had fun times but that was not the reason we were there and especially for Charlie. He wanted to see miracles. He had no interest in talk. He wanted action. He had already known the power of God and he wanted more. So did I. I wanted healing.

Chapter 17

Anything You Ask

Do you want a miracle, Charlie? You can have one. Just wait a while.

Monday night at five o'clock, the familiar Blue Peter tune poured from the television and, crossed legged Charlie and Sam settled down for half an hour of one of their favourite programmes. Drinking tea and dropping cake crumbs all over the carpet, I knew I was guaranteed thirty minutes of quiet and peace. I shut my eyes to soak it in when a loud "Wow look!" jerked me in my comfortable chair.

"Oh no!" "Oh no!" The forthcoming torment was so predictable. I had lived this before and now it was to attack me again. Charlie's whining combined with his stubbornness and refusing to give in were about to batter me again.

"Oh look at them!" shouted the usually quiet Charlie as the new Blue Peter puppies ran riot in the studio. They were adorable golden bundles of fur, tumbling in and out of their baskets whilst the presenters of the programme explained to the viewers all about guide dogs for the blind. I knew exactly what to expect.

"I want a dog," demanded Charlie

"We have talked about this before" I replied firmly," and Dad and I have said "No."

"I want one." The bargaining began. "Why can't I have one?"

"As we've said before, Charlie. Dogs need walks and I can't take a dog for a walk. It would not be a nice life for a dog stuck in the house."

"But I could take him for walks," continued the familiar reasoning.

"No Charlie. You are too young. We have said all this before and that is enough."

"But I want one!" Charlie started to become as ferocious and forceful as he could. "I want one and I want one of those," he demanded pointing at the television as his request became longer and more specific. Never before had he gone as far as choosing the breed of dog. "I'm sorry, Charlie," I explained.

"Those dogs are being trained for helping people who are blind and can't see. You can see and you don't need one. Uncle Jim has made you your nice gold spectacles and you can see. Some people can see nothing at all and they need a dog to help them find their way. In any case, even if you could have a dog there are only a few puppies so there would not be enough for you to have one of those."

"Well I'm going to have one," stated Charlie adamantly. "I'm going to have that one," pointing his sticky finger on to the screen.

"No you are not!" By now, I was beginning to lose my patience.

"Yes I am! I shall ask Jesus for one. He said you can have anything you ask him for," were Charlie's final words as he marched out of the room and stomped up the stairs.

How can a mother explain to her child that when he asks Jesus for something he will not get it? We are told not to destroy a child's faith. In fact, we are told to be like children. I prayed for wisdom.

Charlie said no more and I thought the storm had blown over and he had forgotten. What a relief. Thank you, God!

Sunday morning arrived six days later and we set off for our third week at the new fellowship. It takes me a long time to get to know people and I have a dreadful memory for names. By now, I knew Greg and his wife and could name the Leader, but the others were just a crowd. As the band tuned up, we took our seats at the front so that the boys could see well. The scout hut door was to our left and as we were settling down in walked a couple whose faces were unfamiliar to me. Charlie stopped swinging his legs and reached to the left to feast his eyes on the furry bundle of puppy in their arms. They walked up to Charlie and said

"Look what we've got. She is a Blue Peter puppy and this week she has come to live with us so that we can train her to help blind people. Would you like to stroke her and hold her? She needs to get used to people and noise. Would you like to help us when we bring her to church?"

It was the year that Prince Andrew married and this puppy was called Fergie.

I sat speechless as Charlie stroked and cradled his Blue Peter puppy.

I am still speechless today. Charlie was not at all surprised. It was just so simple. The little boy whose Daddy was a carpenter had kept his promise and given Charlie the puppy he asked for. It was Charlie's miracle, and for a year, he helped and watched Fergie grow and laughed with joy every time he saw his puppy on the television.

Playing with his new furry friend was not to be the only delight for Charlie at the scout hut in the times to come. It seemed to be a church tailor-made for him. There were quizzes, games, competitions, and fun all to be shared with boys of the same age as Charlie and Sam. Last but not least, there were the Hunger Lunches! Hunger Lunches were a new experience for us all.

Meetings were totally unpredictable. We met to see Jesus working and as long as He was doing something we stayed, not because we had to but because we chose to. It was so exciting and there was nowhere else we would rather be. Often the meetings continued longer than an average Anglican service with no pre-arranged order. This gave all the Sunday cooks in the families practical difficulty, but for a mother with my pain and disability, it presented an impossibility. I could not attend the meetings and prepare a Sunday roast dinner. To solve the problem, we changed our plans and Sunday became cheese and biscuits day, or beans on toast day. This is where the Hunger Lunches became such a joy. The idea was that every time it was a Hunger Lunch day, we all gave the money we would have spent on our Sunday lunch to a charity supporting the starving and then we brought to the scout hut some buffet food to share amongst us. In our defence, although we do not need to say this, we gave the cost of the Sunday roast, not the cost of cheese and biscuits. However, what did we receive in return? It was not a lunch. It was a feast! One thing this church knew was how to enjoy food! There were selections of cold meats, various rice salads, garlic bread, green salads, cheese, gateaux, fruit salads, jellies. The choice went on and on. Charlie and Sam had never seen anything like this. We had to hold them back by the back of their trousers to teach considering others first. As the leader thanked Jesus for the abundance he gives us, Charlie and Sam shouted an honest, heartfelt "Amen." Little did they realize that in years to come, the Hunger Lunch was to be a means of God's guidance for them both.

I can say that we got to know Jesus deeper in that place and to see Him at work in our lives. I wish that I could say that we saw miracles and healing every week, or month, or even, in hard times, year, but that was not how it was to be. It would be easy to want to follow a God who gave us all we wanted and who produced a miracle show for our delight, but if that had happened, we would have been there purely for selfish reasons. God wants a relationship with each one of us and it develops as we trust him and use faith. To give us the show we would enjoy would not grow our relationship with him. It is a little like taking your girlfriend to a rock concert every time you meet. You would enjoy it together but you would never get to know her deeply or develop your love.

One thing I learnt about Jesus in our times there was that he always does the unexpected and unpredictable. As soon as you think you have worked him out, he does something totally unexpected. He follows no pattern and cannot be told what to do or be put in a box. Also, he always seems to "come up trumps" when you are at your wits end and are helpless. I suppose that is so that only He can receive the credit. One example was the Blue Peter puppy. Humanly, it was impossible for Charlie to have one but Jesus had a way. His intelligence is far greater than our little minds and his plan way beyond anything we could think in our narrow small parts of life. Another example from scout hut days is the stupid idea of the leader!

One Sunday, our leader asked me if on the following Sunday I would tell the congregation about my illness and how Jesus had not healed me

"How stupid," I thought. What good will that do? It just shows that he does not heal and contradicts what I know by faith is true. Having grown up with no teaching at home or in school about obeying those in authority and choosing to submit to them, I would have said "No," but Jesus was teaching me submission. My lack of respect for John and his authority in our home and my going against his decisions had been something that was a large part of our marriage problems. Also, having parents who were disagreeing over discipline and decisions caused confusion for the boys. Do not misunderstand me. I am of equal value to John and am free to voice my opinions and share in the decisions we make together, but at the end of it all, it is my choice to submit to him and time has proved that this is right. When we disagreed, as we often did, we did it out of earshot of the boys. In their presence, we put up a united front. So, back to the stupid idea. I kept my thoughts to myself and submitted and agreed to give my little talk, leaving Jesus to bail himself out.

To stand at the front and address a group of eighty people was unfamiliar to me, but it was not difficult. I just looked on it as playing another oboe concerto to a packed hall and dealt with it that way.

As I was describing my searing pain and increasing weakness, I noticed a small commotion at the back of the hut. A woman I had never seen before was becoming increasingly upset and a few people were comforting her.

"How amazing," I thought. "That a stranger could feel such compassion for me that she would cry for me."

I concluded that Jesus had not healed me and burbled a bit about multi-vitamins, then went back to my seat. At the end of the meeting, the woman with reddened eyes came towards me and I prepared my body for yet another bruised, painful, Christian hug.

"You have described my illness exactly in detail," she said, still wiping her eyes with a tissue. "What we have is the same. What are we going to do?"

"Keep taking the multi-vitamins," was all I could offer, then remembering Jesus added, "and pray."

"Would you pray for me?" she asked.

Well I could not refuse. Full of no faith whatsoever, I prayed for Jesus to heal her then watched as she walked slowly towards the back of the hut and out of my life. I felt so sorry for her, knowing what a hell this illness is. How sad.

The Bible tells us to rejoice with those who rejoice and mourn with those who mourn. I mourned for her. Eight days later, I cannot honestly tell you that I rejoiced as I received her phone call saying she was pain free and had walked seven miles. I was mightily displeased with God. She was healed and I was still in agony. It took me a few days to get over it. It seemed so unfair. My reaction goes to show how selfish I am. I should have been so happy for her. She came back to the scout hut once and then disappeared from our lives. I wonder, sometimes, if she thanked Jesus and went on to follow him or whether she went away well to a life of pleasing herself. In eternity I shall know, but even then, I knew enough to be able to say that I would rather suffer here for my short time on earth to spend eternity with Jesus and his passionate love for me than to have thirty more years of good health and spend eternity in hell. What an awesome, powerful, all knowing, unpredictable, and exciting God I have. He knows best for us all.

We spent the boys' childhood years at the scout hut and we remember the times there with gratitude and enjoyment. We were so grateful for the church leader there who taught us, advised us, disciplined us, and gave his life to help us. He opened his home to us all, and it is a very special man who would drive five miles in the snow on his motorbike in the dark to answer a cry for help.

It was a time of learning. We learnt about all that Jesus did on earth and witnessed him working today through his spirit. We learnt how he lived his life and how he wants us to live ours. We felt his love for us. We saw him heal people and change people. The John, Pam, Charlie, and Sam who came to the scout hut, left there years later changed people.

I sometimes think children learn more from what they observe around them than from what they are told. Alongside these people, Charlie and Sam saw real life. They saw joy and laughter. They learned to share. They saw adults hurt each other and learnt all about apology and forgiveness. They saw men cry. We lived our lives close to each other everyday, not just on a Sunday, and we knocked the corners off one another. It was not always easy, but the hard times were balanced by hilarious fun. We were always available for one another. In my disability, I was so grateful for the other parents who helped me practically, giving the boys experiences that I was unable to give. One lovely couple took them to London to see the sights (they could write a book about that day. I am not sure they would want to repeat it!). Another mother took them swimming. The scout hut was a perfect situation in which to grow up. There was no confusion for the boys as parents agreed on bringing up our children. Firm lines were set and all the children knew how far they could go. At the same time, they were encouraged to explore and think for themselves. They were allowed to make mistakes and learn from them. They benefited so much from the company of the ten other boys their age and grew in security. In this environment, I could work through my task of setting them free from the wrongs I had grown up with. They were praised not criticized, listened to and made to feel of value. They were accepted with love as they were and had no high expectations to live up to. They were helped to find their strengths and build on them but at the same time recognize their weaknesses and learn how to deal with them. They learnt to have fun even in the hard times.

Chapter 18

The Secret Revealed

One of the most difficult lessons of those years for me was to teach Charlie and Sam to mix with other children and to feel accepted. I had been taught, "Don't bother people. You are a nuisance. Don't get in the way." I was not allowed to have friends to play and rarely allowed to go to friends' homes. Without my life changing experience of Jesus joined to John's different upbringing, this would have been our sons' understanding of life. It is a pack of lies. I had to change that for them but it was so difficult and unnatural for me to trust for their safety as they were out of sight in friends' homes. Also, I hated the noise and mess created by energetic boys bounding around my clean house. I had to change for the sake of Charlie and Sam so that they would learn to make healthy relationships. It was hard and one of my costs of following Jesus. I had to let go control and lose pride. It was a hard ongoing process through which John stood beside me, always supportive and wise.

"Who's coming today?" shouted Sam excitedly as he watched me doing the washing up and resisted picking up a tea towel. From the volume of his voice anyone would have thought we were miles apart not side by side!

"Ben," I replied, trying to sound enthusiastic.

Today was the dreaded day, longed for and so important for the boys, but so hard for me. There was a children's group at the scout hut and once a month one of the boys came to stay overnight. It was everything I hated, noise, mess, a wrecked house, and exhaustion. It was John's idea to encourage friends to stay and I agreed to this. The old Pam would never have entertained even the thought. Yes, Ben is a nice boy but like all boys he is so energetic and loud, just what you do not want when you feel ill. Illness, however, was no excuse. John would be there to help and Charlie and Sam's well-being and right upbringing were my top priority.

Five miles away, Ben was clambering into the old rusty red car, loaded with a duvet and pyjamas. As his parents looked forward to a weekend of peace and quiet, I gritted my teeth and prepared for the hurricane to hit. It was to be the first time Ben had stayed with us and I was not sure what to expect. Driving through the industrial estate and past the Asian shops, the red car and its unknown occupant drew ever nearer. Just as I had no idea what to expect, little did Ben know that he was about to discover the secret of the loft!

Busily, "Ben-proofing" the house, I tried to ignore the signals from my bladder telling me it was over full. With ten minutes before Ben's expected arrival, the bladder won and I sat in the bathroom dealing with it. Men look down, but women look up. Looking at the ceiling I could see the hatch to the loft. I was not conscious of looking at it. I had seen it so many times before but today I had no idea of its significance. It was situated in the right hand corner, a rectangular hatch and not very large. As the population today becomes ever more overweight, I reckon that there would be a large number of people who would be unable to climb through it. It was not designed for today but for thirty years earlier.

When we bought the house, the previous occupants had firmly shut the hatch for ever. It was painted over and was an eyesore. John had plastered over it and the surrounding ceiling and had covered the whole area with stucco that was textured and so, with a layer of white paint, the ceiling looked vaguely respectable. However, knowing that the hatch was there, I could see its shape as a slightly raised rectangular area that visitors would be unlikely to notice. Above it was the loft, its contents and its secret.

Walking, relieved, out of the bathroom, I passed the stair where I used to sit and listen to the little Charlie and Sam having their bedtime conversations. You may have thought that the stair was the top stair of the staircase taking us downstairs, but it was, in fact, the bottom stair of a fully carpeted staircase taking us up to the loft. Today, that was the way into what could have been a useful, large fourth bedroom except that it had no heating and was freezing in winter and boiling in summer. As a room, it was rarely used now and never cleaned. It was to all effects a typical loft but it held the secret about to be discovered.

The doorbell rang and Charlie and Sam fought each other to get to the front door first to welcome in Ben. He stood in the hall, a small blonde boy with a shy sheepish look, taking in his new surroundings. Charlie and Sam bounced excitedly around him and before he could take off his coat or unload his duvet were eagerly escorting him on a tour of their house and showing him the sofa bed on which he would sleep. Ben was quiet, polite, and friendly, but as time went on, Charlie and Sam's excitement began to be infectious and, just as I dreaded, deafeningly noisy boys were careering everywhere, scattering toys, books, and mess all over the place. That was until Ben discovered the stairs to the loft. At that moment in time everything stopped and our lives were to change for years to come.

"What's up here?" called Ben from halfway up the loft stairs.

"Only the loft," I shouted as I made my way up the lower flight of stairs, sensing my need to be there.

"What's in it?" questioned the curious Ben moving a step higher.

"Only a lot of mess and some cases," I answered intending to lure him down to a safer place.

"Can I go in?" Ben's voice was rising and joined by, "Yes let's," chirping from Charlie and Sam who were pushing him upwards from behind. I was about to say "No," when the pressure from Charlie and Sam thrust Ben through the door into the loft. We could all feel the cold air breezing down on us, freshening the warm, cosy central heating.

"Wow!" breathed Ben in a whisper, his mouth open as he surveyed the scene.

Ahead of him at the end of the loft, he could see a small bay window covered in cobwebs. I never cleaned it as it was impossible to walk through the loft because of all the junk. It was a shame because it held a higher view of the rooftops I could see from my bedroom and on a clear day you could see for miles.

Ben's head moved from side to side, his eyes wandering over papers, cases, empty boxes, John's endless files of family history research, Christmas tree decorations, black bin bags, and picture framing equipment. The list of the devastation of the loft could go on for miles and Ben began searching like a starving man would search a tip for a bite to eat. Encouraged by Charlie and Sam, he lay on his stomach grovelling around and chucking pieces of paper behind him.

"Wait a minute," I interrupted, feeling that pit in the stomach I get when things are getting out of my control. Although it was mess beyond anyone's loft mess, it was John's mess. He can create more mess that anyone I know, but to him it is organized mess and he knows exactly where everything is, and woe betide anyone who moves it.

I quickly realized that any words were now in vain as the three boys were oblivious to my presence. There was nothing I could do except watch and try to give a safety warning.

"Be careful, boys. There are things up here you could hurt yourself on. Don't touch Dad's tools or the axe or the guillotine." Images of amputated fingers went through my mind. Shudder!

It was reassuring to hear Charlie, the sensible one, mumble. "We'll be careful." My words had been heard.

By now all that could be seen of Ben were his feet sticking out of a pile of boxes. He felt around, unable to see his way through the heap until his small hand felt a leg. Wiggling sideways he reached to his right where his right hand felt another leg. The loft was about to reveal its secret.

"It's a very old snooker table. No one uses it any more. We just keep things on it," explained Charlie, holding onto Ben's feet.

"Can we use it today?" pleaded Ben. At this point, I heard the distant sound of John's key turn in the front door. Now he could deal with this and take over from me in protecting his precious mess.

Wondering why it was unusually quiet, John came up to see what was going on, only to be faced by three pleading boys wanting to play snooker. They had never shown any interest before. It had needed Ben to be the trigger.

As we had been expecting Ben, John had set aside the weekend for the boys and I was amazed when he agreed to their requests, seeing it as an opportunity for a tidy up. Together they cleared all the boxes and papers off the table to reveal the strong wooden covers that converted the snooker table into an ordinary table. In fact, many years before, we had enjoyed a medieval banquet party on it. With the covers removed it was a sorry sight, with worn out felt and ivory balls whose colours had faded so that they were, apart from the red ones, unidentifiable. This did not deter the boys who set to work with felt tip pens and then grabbed the cues and began trying to hit balls down holes. John loves playing games and was soon involved in teaching the rules of the game and a snooker challenge had begun. Something miraculous was happening. For as far back as I could remember, the boys were quiet. Downstairs enjoying my mug of tea, all I could hear was the plonk of a ball falling through the broken net bags onto the floor and the occasional victorious cheer. They were safe, quiet, and happy.

I told you that this find would change life for us and you must be wondering how one game of snooker would do this, but it was evident, as Ben returned home, delighted with his weekend, that our boys were becoming addicted to the game. When it was clear that this was not just a fad, we decided to restore the old, slate bed, three-quarters snooker table to its former glory. With its wood polished, new felt, mended nets, and coloured balls, it was the focal point of what became a games room. Regularly boys from the scout hut came over to play in the evenings. A graphic artist in the fellowship painted a sign above the table declaring, "Jesus is Lord," and a regular boys group began with John looking after the boys whilst I enjoyed a night out at orchestra. John was really good at this and I would return home to find him exhausted but having really enjoyed himself. In my photo album, I have a lovely photo of Ben hanging up his home-made plaque on the stair wall saying, "This snooker room was opened by Ben Thompson on the 2nd July, 1992."

The news about the wonderful games room began to spread and the boys' school friends started to turn up every Monday, and we had to limit the numbers because of the weight on the loft floor. Charlie and Sam were allowed to choose a few friends each of whom joined the scout hut lads. The loft was bulging on Monday nights and the problem of the limitation of the numbers was naturally solved when winter came and the scout hut lads' parents became reluctant to drive over to us in the cold and dark leaving John with a manageable small local group. It was manageable apart from Dan.

Dan! Mmmm! My God-given task was to teach the boys truth, let go of all controlling in their lives and give them freedom. This was to be a real test for me. If I could have been controlling Dan would most definitely not been in one of the groups. He would not have been allowed in our house. It was D for Dan and D for disruptive. However, Charlie really liked him and wanted to include him. I voiced my concerns to John who said he was prepared to take responsibility for this boy, adding that if he was not in our loft, he could be somewhere else doing something far less desirable. So I submitted to that and left John with the consequences of his decision.

Dan was taller than the others, with a cheeky grin, and he was to test John to his limits. John is a very patient man, but Dan tried his patience time and time again. I would return from my rehearsal to find John sitting with his head in his hands, exhausted. After a pleasant evening tooting my way through some Mozart, I was greeted as I walked through the door by a roaring, "That's his last chance. Next time he's banned!"

The next time was the memorable evening when Charlie and Sam poured through the front door before I could open it, obviously in deep distress. The story according to them was confirmed by John. Dan had been at his worst that evening, driving John to tear out his hair. Eventually, it had all become too much for John. The final straw came when Dan stood up to his tallest and pointed a finger at the "Jesus is Lord" sign declaring, "I am a Satanist."

Dan had gone too far. He had crossed the line. John was overcome with rage and murder came to mind. God was gracious in that Dan lived, but the horror of what was to come remains in the memories of all those present. John strode over to Dan, placed a firm hand on each of his shoulders, put his nose two inches away from Dan's nose, and prayed loudly at him. Even worse, he prayed a stream of foreign words in his God-given language at the hapless Dan who was stunned into terrified silence. Boys were falling about the loft in helpless laughter and Charlie and Sam were cowering under the snooker table in embarrassment, wondering how they could ever face their friends again. John was shocked and so was Dan. Thankfully, after a week's rest, everyone had recovered and John chose to demonstrate the forgiveness of God by allowing Dan back into the group on condition that he behaved.

The small group of school friends grew up to be a group of young men who got together most Sunday nights for a pint in the local pub. Charlie was always there, loving their company and sharing their lives. He constantly prayed for them all. Some of them took manual jobs after leaving school and Dan went to work for a brewery, loading barrels into pub cellars.

Dressed in his suit ready for work one Monday, Charlie said, "Dan hasn't been to the pub for some weeks now. I must check that he's not in trouble." Charlie rarely moves fast and after some weeks he had not checked on Dan.

Some days for me are "bed bad days" and on one such Saturday, Charlie burst into the bedroom shouting, "I knew I should have checked on Dan. I've just had a call from him and he says that he's met Jesus and has been going to church and not to the pub. He's asked me to go to his baptism!" My mind boggled and I was thinking the same as Charlie.

"I want to go and check on this," continued Charlie. "I'll go and see him tomorrow morning and find out what has happened."

The next morning "in bed" was the last place I wanted to be. Charlie set off for Dan's saying to John,

"I'll phone if he's in trouble. If I don't phone meet me at the Christian Centre for Dan's baptism."

All day Charlie was gone and we waited for the phone call. By six o'clock it had not come and so, as agreed, John set off to meet Charlie at the Christian centre.

"It's true, it's real," said Charlie as they entered the church. There at the baptismal pool, they watched in amazement as a glowing Dan spoke of meeting a Jesus of passionate love and of how the experience had changed him for ever. It was evident for all to see. He had repented and totally changed. My phone did not ring, but someone's did and guess whose! It was Charlie's mobile that rang right in the middle of the baptism! Quietly leaving the room, Charlie answered his phone to find that the callers were his mates from school wanting to know why he was not at the pub. When he told them he was in church at Dan's baptism, their response was as incredulous as mine and everyone who knew Dan. After the service, a wet Dan came up and hugged John and said, "Thank you for praying in tongues for me that night. I never forgot it."

Where do you find Dan now? In pubs! You cannot miss him. He is the tall young man telling everyone enthusiastically about his wonderful Jesus.

I conclude that we see the outside of people and make our judgements, but God knows their hearts, their potential, and their part in his plan. He knew Dan and loved him when I would have rejected him. Jesus is Lord.

Chapter 19

Surely Not Here?

As we saw the need that the local lads had for the games night, so we saw the need amongst our neighbours, friends, and families for a local fellowship. Somewhere Jesus was free to do as He wanted and people were free to enjoy sharing lives, love, and experiencing all Jesus wanted to give them. We remembered the amazing times we had shared with our friends years ago when the boys were small and longed for the excitement of seeing the supernatural miracles amongst us once more. It was fine for us to go to the scout hut, but it was becoming apparent that there was a local need. Having discussed this with Greg and the leaders of the fellowship, we set aside every Thursday night to pray for this and ask Jesus to show us what He wanted. Within a week, an old lady heard of our prayers and came to join us. She may have been old but she had experienced the power of God and was not prepared to settle for religion. She wanted action. We became quite excited and imagined flocks of like minded people queuing up outside our house every Thursday night. As usual it did not work out as we hoped and the three of us carried on alone.

In bed at night, waiting for sleep, my imagination wandered over thoughts of what God would do. I knew, from past experience, that He would do something but what? Perhaps, we would buy the upper floor of the small local Co-op supermarket and strip and paint it. It would have a modern pale green carpet and soft lighting. The news of wonderful miracles would spread around the area and flocks of people desperate for healing would come. Or perhaps, we would hire the local primary school and there would be rooms for the little children to play and enjoy the fun that Charlie and Sam had at the scout hut whilst at the same time getting to know Jesus.

As always, God's plans are not Pam's plans. His are perfect but until later always seem almost crazy to my human mind. I mean, "Why did He choose Dan!"

Within a year, we had the answer to our prayers and it almost horrified me. It came to our notice that a nearby Baptist Church was buying a disused and closed down old Methodist church to open for the local area.

"What! A church!" That's the last place I had wanted. It felt religious and a real turn off.

"I think we should go and see what is going on," insisted John

"But that's not what we wanted," I bleated.

"It may be what God wants," John persisted

"Huh!" I thought silently to myself, trying to avoid a sulk and to maintain a positive attitude in front of the boys. "Let's judge it at the end I suppose."

"We're just going for this Sunday to see what is going on," I explained to Charlie and Sam, trying to sound encouraging whilst they were puzzled as to why we were not going to the scout hut as usual.

"I'll miss Ben today," whined Charlie, putting on his trainers.

"Just today." I emphasized. "You'll see Ben next week."

We could have walked if I was able but we climbed into the car and parked in the nearby pub car park. There were a few cars parked along the roadside and I wondered what their owners inside the church were like.

My horror grew as I saw the church. It was made of old charcoal grey stone and slates were falling off the roof. Its filthy stained glass windows were covered in rusty wire netting to try to prevent vandalism and ancient stone gravestones were buried in overgrown grass. Its old wooden doors, which had been closed for years, were slightly ajar and the broken toilets were outside and up a slippery path. The whole impression of the place spelt "dead!" In fact, the only sign of life was a small woolly goat tethered to one of the gravestones. It was his job to munch the grass and keep it down.

I pushed Charlie and Sam inside where a large motherly woman welcomed us and gave us a green news sheet and I shuddered as we sat down on a row of dark wooden pews and observed the plaster falling off the walls.

"I'm freezing," moaned Charlie.

"It won't be for long," I reassured him. "Soon the heating will come on."

And it did! Long metal pipes along the pews started to warm up producing a horrible stinking smell of burning rubber as the soles of my boots started to melt and stick to them.

Suddenly, a guitar and keyboard began to play and a lady took her place on a stage covered with a threadbare carpet. Wearing a bright cheerful green jumper and a cheerful smile to match it, she threw her arms out widely and began to sing loudly and with great enthusiasm.

"Fling wide the gates. Let the King come in."

"I wouldn't come in here if I was him," I thought as my mouth sung the words projected on the overhead screen.

No one in their right mind would come in here let alone
Almighty God. I did have to admit, though that in my
experience and that of others, Jesus turns up in the most
unexpected places, in terraced houses, in bathroom show-
ers, in university lecture theatres. He can be anywhere, so
I suppose He might turn up in this derelict place. I could
not imagine what was going on in the minds of the leaders
of the Baptist church, when they decided to buy this place.
It seemed to me that the only thing going for it was its
position. I never wanted to go again. Why leave our cosy,
supportive friends and uproot the boys from their secure
place? I was confident that John would feel the same and so,
breathing a sigh of relief, I headed for the car carrying my
green notice sheet.

"Charlie and Sam deserve medals for tolerating that," I
whispered to John out of their earshot.

"Mmm," was his worrying response. I had heard that
before and it meant that he was thinking. I was not even
prepared to think about thinking of returning.

Sitting with our plates of cheese and biscuits on our
knees, I waited for the boys' response. They munched
and said nothing, probably because they thought that they
would only go once. I chose to keep my negative thoughts
to myself and see what John would say. He kept just as quiet
too as he relived the morning in his mind.

I had only just opened my mouth when John interrupted
with his

"We can't judge this on just one visit. We need to go
again."

"Again!" I spluttered. "Again!"

"Yes," John was adamant. "People need this and yes,
there will need to be a lot of work but look at its position
on the hill. We need to go back."

"But think….."

"Pam, you're thinking of us and what we want. It's about what God wants. You haven't even looked at the notice sheet yet."

Reluctantly, I turned over the sheet and began to read it. It contained information that I had not expected or could have imagined. The wreck of a former glorious church was to be run alongside the Baptist church who now owned it as it was being restored. That would mean that we would be moving to and fro between buildings, something I had never considered. I did not want to be messing around like this. I hated change at the best of times and it is hard enough to be getting involved in anything when you are ill and this just looked like too much. My face said it all, but John was now not a man to be manipulated or controlled and neither did I want to do so. My life's purpose was to make a turn around in my generation, freeing the boys to find God and who they really were. It was not to persuade them to do as I wanted and make them male replicas of myself and my ancestors. I knew I had to submit. I had to go back and I had to encourage Charlie and Sam when I least felt like it.

"God might be wanting us to go there," I told the boys. " We must go because Dad wants to make sure what God wants."

"Won't we go to the scout hut?" asked Sam. "I'll miss my friends."

"I think we should go back to the scout hut next week and then back up the road the week after. We could alternate for a while until we get a clear view of their vision and God's plan," advised John wisely.

I do not think the boys could fully understand what he had said. To Sam he was reassured that he would see his friends next week and who could know the mind of Charlie? He would always see things in a different way from everyone else and would be thinking deep thoughts for a long time that young boys do not usually think.

"Can I see the notice sheet?" asked Charlie, peering over my shoulder. We looked at it together and I began to read the small section entitled "Forthcoming events."

"Let's see what's happening in two weeks time," I suggested, trying to sound positive. "My goodness. You'll never guess what's going to happen. It's a Hunger Lunch at the Baptist church."

A hunger lunch. Oh joy of joys! All hearts leapt at the thought.

"That's two hunger lunches in two weeks," counted Charlie, whose maths was far better than his reading.

"A hunger lunch!" cheered Sam dancing around the room.

Now there was a reason for returning once more and hope returned.

Feasting in the scout hut the following Sunday, we recounted our gruesome experience to Greg as Charlie and Sam munched their way through scotch eggs and garlic bread.

"I think I'll make a black forest trifle for next week," I thought to myself looking ahead. It was easy to make, looked good, and tasted delicious. I thought it would bless these friendly strangers with its whipped cream topping covered in cherries and scattered chocolate flake. I talked over my choice with Sam who joined in my enthusiasm, not because he liked black forest trifle but because anything chocolate was irresistible to him, (and still is today as he comforts himself whilst commuting into the financial centre of London with his chocolate ration and laptop. I love you, Sam!)

Full to bursting, we travelled home to live another week and look forward to God's goodness. The week passed quickly and soon I was breaking up squares of black cherry jelly and the big Sunday arrived. Carrying the jelly carefully, we shivered our way through another dark, dismal ninety minutes and then leapt into the car and moved at speed for the Hunger lunch. The Baptist church was a beautiful sight with its car park full of cars and its bright notices outside. It was relatively modern and very comfortable. As my walking was limited, John dropped me and the boys outside the door whilst he parked the car. Entering the front doors, we instantly felt welcome and I held out my trifle as an offering to the lady in the church porch. Her response to my loving gesture was puzzling but polite as she directed us through to the main meeting room. This was a church but it did not feel "churchy." The room was bright and chairs were scattered randomly. The walls were adorned with embroidered banners and there was a buzz of activity around.

"I'll take it into the kitchen," replied the helpful young woman and I watched as she carried it through a door into a room beyond.

"Where is the Hunger Lunch?" squeaked Sam, his intelligence already at work as he observed the absence of food in the main hall.

"I don't know," I whispered. "We'll try to find out," looking for a way of asking the whereabouts of the food whilst trying not to appear to be there for the food!

"Where is lunch?" I asked casually.

"It will be later in the room off the kitchen," I was informed.

I repeated the necessary information to the boys as John entered the main room just in time for one of the leaders to stand on the stage and say

"Lord, we thank you for the abundance of food you give to us. Help us never to forget the millions who are starving."

This was the signal for the stampede into the kitchen and gradually a queue was formed. We did not want to appear too eager and held the boys back, joining the queue approximately twelve people from the front. Ahead of us was a clean but small modern kitchen adjoining a long rectangular room containing groups of chairs and small Formica-topped tables. Two long trestle tables rested along the length of the room and held the lunch, but what lunch? On the kitchen work surface was an enormous pot of vegetable soup, and sixty plates of food were prepared and waiting on the tables. As we neared the front of the queue, the feast met our eyes. Each plate held a chunk of bread, a small square of cheese, and a windfall apple. Where our trifle went to I shall never know.

Balancing bowls of soup in one hand I gave Charlie and Sam their plates which they received in silence. This was a Hunger Lunch.

"I don't think God wants us in this church," whispered Sam, looking woefully down at his plate and trying to find a part of his apple without a bruise from which to take a bite.

"Nor do I!" echoed Charlie adamantly and with authority.

That day we all learned about hunger and not only did the boys have to suffer this painful lesson but they also had to endure a sixty-minute video about the charity they were supporting.

Hungry and downcast, we drove them home to be comforted with beans on toast as we explained that this really was the meaning of hunger lunches. That day we were grateful for our simple lunch.

Children are very capable of manipulating their parents. Charlie and Sam had learnt obedience and would follow as we asked, but in this case, they would have made their feelings very clear and did so for a whole two weeks. However, all was not lost. From behind the pot of soup a pair of dark brown bright eyes had watched the distraught Sam and taken pity. The lady they belonged to took the trouble to find our telephone number and invite us to lunch after the next Sunday ordeal.

When the day arrived, Charlie and Sam moaned and groaned, whined and protested questioning John's decision all the way to the church. We dragged them in with the promise of lunch with a new friend, which did little to silence them. With his bottom lip pouting out, Sam prepared himself for another rotten apple, and two reluctant boys were welcomed into a warm and comfortable bungalow. I now know that this lady (a dear and faithful friend for many years) lived a life of prayer and she must have had a hot line to God. Sitting politely on best behaviour, Sam was served the largest plate of lamb in his lifetime, with enough mint sauce for drowning his meal. A large smile grew as he suddenly saw our situation in a new way. For Sam, God had changed his mind and did want us in this church. He would put up with anything for lamb and mint sauce and spent the next week persuading Charlie that God blesses obedience.

Chapter 20

Christmas Peace

After several months and a lot of prayer, John was convinced that we should leave the scout hut and support this local church. I was not sure. It was so different from any of my imaginings, but as John led I followed. I looked on the move as a costly sacrifice on my part, losing close friends, security, and comfort. I was moving for the sake of local neighbours and children. That was how I viewed it. God, however, knows our future and He could see it in a different way. He was moving us for our sakes, and particularly the sakes of Charlie and Sam.

By now, the little boys in duffel coats had grown into taller boys in short jackets, with gelled hair. God had asked me to release them into freedom and that meant a gradual freeing from me and my opinions and desires. It was important that they were free to explore. I knew that the last thing God wanted was for them to be brain-washed into copying our beliefs. He wanted them to find a deep relationship with him. He wanted more than to share one breakfast with Charlie and that meant, "Mum, get out of the way!" This was to turn out to be the perfect environment for this freeing as the youth work took place in the modern Baptist Church whilst we beavered away helping to practically prepare a place for Jesus in the other church. Charlie and Sam were free and provided with young people in their twenties to help them learn. The other young boys and girls quickly included them in their lives although they attended different schools and they were eager to be with them. The tyres on our car needed more regular replacing as we journeyed backwards and forwards between the two places. Every parent of young teenagers knows the taxi driver feeling!

Sam was still in his last year at junior school and had to cope with not just a major move to a senior school but the church move as well. It was a lot for Sam who at that time needed security. Eleven-year-old boys do not want Mummy to take them to their new school on their first day and that first day took courage for Sam. However, it was accept-able to be accompanied by another older pupil and so, as through all the junior years, it was Charlie who took him and helped to settle him in.

As any mother is concerned for their growing son, my concern was rather overshadowed by my concern for my father. It was not concern for his continuing involvement in freemasonry and his spiritual life. It was concern for his health. I knew Jesus had placed Fred in his life and that all was safe in God's hands. I did not have to worry, but his health was a growing concern.

Father was not old but he retired from general practice early whilst continuing to serve the community in other ways. I was glad that he would have more free time and pleased to see him enjoying lunching with friends and using his passion for Delia Smith to take over in the kitchen. Sadly though, the man God had used to bring physical comfort and healing to so many was becoming unwell. He battled on, serving others, but you did not have to be medically qualified to notice the changes. The vegetable plot that he loved to tend before morning surgery was being neglected. He only had to lift a hose pipe and gout developed in his wrist. He was changing shape and becoming more like "Whinnies-the-Pooh." The legs that sprinted up twenty flights of stairs to save a life on the top storey of a block of flats when the lift broke down were now becoming bowed. More concerning was his breathlessness and small cough that drove my mother round the bend with irritation and worry. One lunchtime he took us to a Chinese restaurant and I was shocked to see that his skin was more yellow than that of the waiters. He had contracted two different types of hepatitis during his working life, and the jaundice showed that his liver was not happy.

Here God put us in this church for our sakes. The Baptist church was halfway between our house and my father's bungalow and so it was easy for us to call in often. Yes, we had to cut ourselves off from his masonic activities and minimise negative input, but we loved him dearly and visited as much as we could.

Father was always very generous and particularly so on my birthday. He gave me so much and I gave so little. In June, before the start of the school year, I took Sam to see him thinking that Sam would have less time in the autumn. Immediately we arrived, Grandpa hit the kitchen and beef sandwiches appeared as if from nowhere. As Sam was eating, Father called me into his study and gave me my birthday present. I kissed him and said nothing but he could not have missed the tears welling up in my eyes. He was mentally sound and no idiot. My birthday was not until October.

"Is he dying?" I asked one of his medical partners.

"Most certainly not!" was the shocked reply.

I was not so certain.

On my birthday, I sat on his hospital bed.

"You didn't expect to be here on my birthday," I mentioned, trying to sound casual.

"No," he replied, but that was the end of the conversation. As always, he was more concerned for others than for himself and his mind was on the fact that his dear friend, Fred, was also in a different hospital.

Being ill myself made hospital visiting difficult and it was a relief when he returned to the bungalow after just one week.

As he slept more on the large velvet sofa, so the front garden began to change. It was a little like a smaller version of the flowers laid after Princess Diana's death, yet he had not died. His patients were doing their best to heal their beloved doctor. There was not one who did not regard him as the solution to all their problems and an adopted member of their family. He had all his life worked amongst the Asian community and the poor and now mangoes were piling up in mountains against the rockery.

"Mangoes good for healing," we were told.

Long before restaurants delivered takeaways, curries were filling the kitchen to make him well.

"Curry has no chilli. Chilli bad for heart." They all tried to save him.

Autumn leaves fell and frosty days began. Sam had a half-mile walk to and from school and he was flagging. He looked pale and tired. All the new changes and a long term were pushing him to exhaustion. Everyday he took his chocolate out of his advent calendar and counted the days to his holiday. Two more days to go. That meant only two days in which I had some peace to prepare for Christmas. I loved to sit by the Christmas tree, with the lights of the room turned off and just the magical lights of the tree twinkling. As I relaxed and gazed at them, I became a child again, but only for a short time. There! I had done it again. That annual sin for which I had not repented. I had eaten all the chocolates on the tree. I could not blame it on Sam. It was I who was to blame. I had only two days in which to replace them before John noticed.

I was about to leave the house when the doorbell rang. There was my father holding a small gift-wrapped present.

"Happy Christmas," he said offering it to me.

"Oh, please come in," I begged. I was so happy to see him.

"No. I must go. I have a lot of people to see," he answered firmly. He had always been so short of time when visiting the many patients everyday that he never in retirement got used to spending long in any house.

I wanted to be with him so I followed him to the car where my mother was ready to drive him to the next visit. He turned round and spoke to me with that voice that I had always obeyed as a child.

"Go in! It's freezing and slippery out here. Go in!"

I did as I was told and waved goodbye from the house. It was only a short interruption to my day but during that time I decided to postpone my shopping trip until tomorrow.

Later that evening, I waited to see if John had noticed the absence of chocolates on the tree. It looked as if my crime was to remain undiscovered but, yet again, God had a different plan.

"I think I will take tomorrow off," announced John.

It is for some reason so infuriating. He always does this just before Christmas when I am up to my eyes in work, changing my plans and getting under my feet! It was so near to Christmas that I had forgotten about it and not allowed a spare day.

"Do you have to? It's such a busy time?" I pleaded.

"I can help," said John.

That would be even worse. I am sure many women can identify with my feelings.

"Perhaps you might enjoy pottering round the shops and seeing the decorations," I suggested, trying to rescue my time.

"We'll see," was John's vague reply.

It was at this point in the conversation that I remembered the chocolates. I was bound to be found out. I spent the evening trying to rearrange the following day and decided, not being a "morning person" to get up early and rescue the chocolate situation before John was awake enough to notice.

"Last day," cheered Sam as I kissed him goodbye. He so much needed that holiday. As soon as he had left, I put on my coat and was about to open the front door when the telephone rang. I decided to answer it so that John was not woken. It was my mother calling early.

"I'm sorry your father died last night," she said faintly.

"I only saw you yesterday!"

A cold shiver went down my back leaving a numbness in my head. I could not think. My mind went blank.

"Are you on your own?" I asked.

"No, Jess (the daily help) is here."

"Can I speak to her please?"

The phone was handed over to Jess.

"I'm coming over as soon as I can. Could you stay fifteen minutes until I get there?"

"I'll do anything," sobbed Jess, a faithful friend who loved them dearly and helped them in many ways beyond her job required.

By now John was at the top of the stairs, aware that something unusual was going on.

"My Dad's dead," was all I could say.

He rushed down the stairs and threw an arm around me and then, typical of him, said exactly what I needed.

"What do you want me to do?"

"I think I want you to go out for fifteen minutes and leave me in the house on my own; then come back and take me to the bungalow please," was my instinctive response.

John turned around to go back upstairs and stopped halfway. I was so grateful that he was with me. As so often, God was ahead of me in this, providing all I needed. John turned round and looking down at me said gently

"Pam, I don't want you to worry that he hadn't seen Fred."

"HADN'T SEEN FRED!" That was the last thing I had been thinking of. Now numbness turned to hysterical panic as I remembered the specific words in my dream.

He hadn't seen Fred.

The dream was from the devil to shut me up so he never heard of Jesus.

I had believed a lie.

He had not repented or renounced his freemasonry.

He had gone to hell.

I was devastated. John, by now dressed, helpfully went out as I threw myself onto the sofa and let out a scream that could have been heard throughout a ten mile radius. I howled into a cushion and then ran to the fridge and ate all the brandy butter. By the time John returned I had pulled myself together and was ready to go to support my mother.

A red-eyed Jess let us in and my mother was sitting upright in her knitting chair, her hands clasped together, trembling, in her, "I am on my best behaviour" pose. I went to put my arms around her but she pushed me away, knowing that any demonstration of love would have caused her to fall apart. I held Jess instead before thanking her and saying we would be alright. I sat in the chair as near to my mother as she would have felt comfortable.

"What happened?" I asked as gently as I could, trying to disguise my rising panic.

In a calm but faint voice she recounted the painful hours she had been through.

"He said he felt unwell and went to bed early. In the night his breathing changed. I asked him if I should call an ambulance and he refused. It must have been shortly after that that he died."

There was so much more that I wanted to ask such as, "What were his last words to you," but I knew it was too much.

A few minutes silence followed and then mother's expression changed to a puzzled, bemused look.

"I can't understand it," she puzzled. "He seemed well. We delivered presents and when we came home Fred arrived. He had just been discharged from hospital. They spent about two hours talking in the study while I cooked a meal. He ate a good meal and do you know what he did? He thanked Jesus for the food and prayed before we started to eat. It was so unlike him and he seemed so well. It's such a shock."

This was just what I needed to hear and joy and peace flooded my whole being. The dream was from God. Dad was safe. All was well.

Before I met Jesus I would say my Father was my God. That had to change and it did, but God knew how much I loved my Father and how I would not have ever been able to cope with his death on my own. God enabled me to handle the impossible through his revelation years earlier in my dream and my seeing his revealed plan working out.

There was so much to do, driving around, visiting the funeral director, comforting devastated people, and telephoning. I lost count of the number of cups of coffee I made. Miles away Jim was packing for a three-hour journey to help. A tsunami had hit our Christmas. It had washed it all away. The tree meant nothing, we could not care about food, tinsel and lights looked ridiculous. Christmas had been stripped away. But we were left with our focus on a baby in a manger who came to promise that death is not the end and to give us eternal life.

By three o'clock, we were exhausted and having a quick cup of tea before facing the boys.

"I've eaten all the tree chocolates" I confessed.

"I know;" John was smiling.

"And all the brandy butter," I dared to add.

"It's OK."

How I love my husband. He's a tower of strength to me in the hardest of times, a gift to me from God.

We heard the key in the door and I rushed to get there to meet the boys.

"Yippee!" screamed Sam. "It's Christmas!" He sprang through the door, his eyes shining and a grin from ear to ear as he let off a party popper. How on earth could I tell him? I herded them into the lounge with John and sat them down. It seemed at the time that the best way was to keep it simple and see what happened. We were, after all, taking the day a few minutes at a time.

"Grandpa's died." It was so simple. I waited for their reactions. I knew Charlie would be placid and calm, but I could never have anticipated his reaction. Sitting bolt upright he asked.

"What is the date?"

"It's the 22nd of December." I answered, wondering what was going on in his head.

"22nd of December," he stated forcefully. "I'll go and write it on the family tree."

He passed the silent Sam as he headed for the loft. Sam was the noisy one and I expected his response to be dramatic and loud, but he said nothing. Suddenly he raced after Charlie, passing him on the stairs and leapt onto his bed, diving under his duvet and refusing to come out. That was where he wanted to be and so there we left him.

There was so much to do and Charlie asked so many questions. Sam stayed under his duvet refusing all food and hiding himself. Twenty four hours later, he was still there and it was necessary for us to go out to meet Jim in the evening. I wanted to be there for Sam, but I had to go. Sam was very close to my young cousin and so we left her to comfort him and pressed on with the job.

When we returned, she had coaxed Sam downstairs and he sat in silence by the fire. The next day was Christmas Eve, when we had always enjoyed a family evening meal out. We needed to eat so we decided to go but at the start of the day, just to add to the complications, Sam was ill. He looked grey and screamed and writhed on the sofa clutching his stomach. He was obviously in great pain but we were reluctant to call out a doctor on Christmas Eve. Time was not healing and thoughts of an appendicitis crossed my mind. We could not leave it. A doctor soon came and was most kind and caring. On examining Sam he could find nothing specifically wrong and we concluded it was a shock reaction. Everyone went for their Christmas meal but I could not leave Sam. In any case, I was not very hungry and a quiet night was quite appealing.

Sam seemed to settle a little and I stroked his hair as I put him in bed. I turned off all the lights except the tree and enjoyed a glass of sherry and a chocolate mint. It seemed so crazy that my dearest Father had died and I was overflowing with joy. He was no more dead than his father and mother. They are alive and we are only separated by time.

We talked to Jim and all agreed that the funeral service should be as our mother wanted. We did, however, make it clear to Jim, who fully understood and accepted our beliefs, that it was to be a Christian service. Freemason friends were dropping envelopes of suggested Masonic hymns and prayers through the letterbox, but we ignored them. Jesus was to be at the centre of the service and that was our mother's wish too.

At the large old Norman church at least four hundred people gathered. It was hard to take it all in. Immaculately dressed Masonic women sat side by side with dirty, poverty-struck patients in threadbare clothes. Saris mingled with black suits and voices of all faiths united to sing with such volume.

"Thine be the glory, risen conquering Son.

Endless is the victory thou over death has won."

For so many people there my Father was God. It was to him that they all turned for advice, comfort, and help in trouble. It had to change and God needed Jesus to take his rightful place in their lives. They left that service in no doubt that they had a choice to make. In a couple of weeks, Jim chose Jesus and his choice was made wonderful by his wife's personal experience of that passion I sometimes felt. In her sadness and mixed emotions she met Jesus halfway down their stairs.

We have a truly wonderful God.

I held Fred's cold hand outside the church and for the first time told him about my dream. He was not surprised and just said reassuringly

"Your father knew the way and he took it."

After the cremation, we gathered at the bungalow for the largest joint of beef I have ever seen. He had always said he wanted beef sandwiches after his funeral. I have never seen so many grown men cry and I was told people's individual stories of love he had given in so many ways and about which he had said nothing. I could recount them all, but this is a book about Jesus who gave him the love he shared so generously.

It was at the beef sandwich time that I learnt the diagnosis of Sam's dreadful pain. My cousin had coaxed him out from under the duvet by offering him a chocolate cream egg. As this seemed to be helping him, she assisted him in consuming twelve of them. Greed Sam? You suffered the consequence of sin!

It may sound ridiculous but I remember that Christmas as being the best and most meaningful Christmas I have ever had. Stripped of the trash, it was all about Jesus and love. It was about God's love for us and our human love for one another expressed in hugs, words, tears, and closeness. United by loss we were united in love. Especially for me, it was about my father's love for me. Jesus said we should pray to "Our Father, who art in Heaven." The love my father gave me has been an earthly demonstration of a God of abundant generosity, a God who disciplines us, a God who knows us inside out.

A few days after the funeral, I decided it was time to open the gift my father had given me as I saw him for the last time. I wanted it to be a private moment and not part of the family present opening. It was small, hard, and heavy. A most generous Father, he always spent an unnecessary amount of money on me at Christmas. What had he bought me as his final gift to me? I took off the label on which he had written

"To Pam, Love Daddy."

I keep it in my "happy box." Could it be expensive perfume? I shook it but it was not liquid. Gold jewellery had often been my gift but this was obviously not in a box. It was unusual. The only way to find out was to unwrap it. Slowly, I removed the holly berry paper to reveal his last gift to me. It was a jar of brandy butter. Yes, he knew me so well. He knew he was dying and he knew one of the first things I would do would be to scoff the brandy butter. He had replaced it for me and demonstrated how deeply and well God knows and loves me.

Chapter 21

Feeling Pale

Do you know how it feels to be exhausted, worn out, and "at the end?"

They did, bless them. At the end of the shelf, Easter Chicken sat flopping, his bright yellow fur a dirty greyish green, his glass eyes scratched, and his beak hanging on by a thread. Against him lay Scotty Bear, much thinner now and threadbare, his glorious tartan paws frayed. For them, the fighting was over. The young boys who owned them were teenagers now. They were retired but "Burrr" was an unforgettable word in our memories.

Whilst John sweated sanding wooden floors in the dark old church and giving his all to help restore it, the boys luxuriated in the warm, bright, modern Baptist church. There they could ask all their questions and receive advice from the young leaders without parents looking nervously over their shoulders. We were letting them gradually go free.

They enjoyed the blastingly loud music and the thudding drum beat. They made friends away from us.

As they settled into their church and we beavered away in ours, because of the link of a joint leadership and the joining of the two churches we got to know their friends' parents and they became friends. We were so grateful for their love, support, and advice as we made our way through our bereavement. They tried their best to understand my neurological illness and often had the boys to stay. My mother never recovered from my father's death and as her health declined, they helped support me as I did my best to care for her until she also died two years later. The demands on me in those four years worked in Charlie and Sam's favour as I could not be in two places at one time and so, as I cared for her I had less time to be watching over them. Many parents were standing over their youngsters, supervising coursework and pressuring, but I could not do that. It was making it easier for me to work towards my goal of setting Charlie and Sam free from my control, although it was a hard way to have to take.

John and I united to free them and as soon as they were legally allowed to be left on their own, we took the unusual step of telling them that they did not have to go to church any more. We wanted them to find Jesus themselves and follow him not us. Charlie, of his own choice, regularly went every Sunday and often to the weekday evening meetings. We saw him read his Bible and search for truth. Occasionally, I clambered over his junk in order to attempt to dust his room and found the little prayers that he had written down. Charlie was a thinker (in the words of one of his close friends, "he out thinks himself,"). He even requested the X-rays from the hospital as he remembered his leg lengthening miracle. He was on his way.

Sam took a different path. It was not so easy for him as he was two school years younger than Charlie was and there were only three teenagers of his age. Soon the comfort of a warm Sunday lie in became irresistible and gradually he left and made friends outside of church at school. Charlie never became religious or "churchy" and had many friends outside of church. It was a healthy situation for them both. At school they mixed with others of many different faiths to learn about and consider and they were free to do so.

After selling my mother's bungalow and dealing with all that follows a death, we breathed a sigh of relief and hoped to spend more time as a family. We were to do this but not in a way to aid my healing as I had hoped. Within a year, John became ill. All he could say was that he felt "pale." His blood tests were showing bizarre results and yet despite many visits to different hospital departments, his illness was undiagnosed. The past came back to haunt me. As the news of the devastation of aids hit news headlines daily, I sat in dread and terror. In the previous months one of his friends had died of AIDS and although he was in no way involved sexually with John, I shivered until the test result was clear. I am grateful for God's mercy. To have to suffer this extra consequence of his actions would have been so hard on me.However, what was to come was hard enough.

We entered the small consulting room to be greeted by a young lady doctor. She looked so young that I guessed that she had recently qualified and so her investigations and unexpected results surprised me. We had prayed to know what was wrong and the answer was to come through her.

"Please sit down," she gestured. "I had a hunch," she continued.

"I had seen this once in medical school and the MRI scan I ordered has confirmed this. What is wrong is very serious but I have a plan."

I shall never forget those words. How wise they were. They told the truth but gave hope.

"You have kidney cancer."

John was silent and I, having grown up in a doctor's house, found it easier to understand the details and the plan.

Once more the family was hurtled back into hospital life as John, Jesus, the doctors and their teams fought for his life.

Charlie and Sam became strong supports for me and I cannot thank the church enough for their care at that time. It is the small things that counted. I remember one man coming to visit and humbly holding a gift.

"It's some Brie cheese that you like," he said, offering it to John and placing a caring hand on his shoulder. It may have been a lump of cheese but it was his love. He brought his love and love carried us through. Thankfully, eleven years later, John is still here.

For Charlie and Sam, their teenage years were hospital, funeral, hospital, funeral, hospital. All they achieved they did so through their own efforts. All credit goes to them. I could only stand and observe them as they made their way through, and provide the much needed "swot pots" of dolly mixtures, chocolate buttons, and wine gums at revision times. As my God-given task was not to control them, it was the teenage years that would have been the most potentially damaging times for them. All was made easier by my absences. The way each of them chose to go was so different from the way I would have thought best and as John supported them and I submitted to him, they found God's best way.

Sam was obviously a gifted musician and as a musician myself, knowing the pleasure, I took from music, I would have pushed him that way. I cried my tears in the privacy of my bedroom as he chose to terminate his music lessons and move into business studies and computing. He was the one who helped me so much practically at home, carrying in heavy shopping for me. I agonized as he left home to go to university. I needed him so much. I remember going to the toilet in the middle of the night just after he left. The street light outside cast a beam of light across an empty bed and I cried my eyes out. I still do not leave that door open at night. Today, I am so rewarded as I see his success and satisfaction in his work.

Charlie was always sewing and knitting! He was very practical and found reading and studying difficult. I would have encouraged him into a practical job such as upholstering. However, Charlie chose to begin his career by licking envelopes in the local town hall. From there he worked voluntarily for an accountants office then taking temporary jobs in finance. Not discouraged by frequent redundancies, he worked in the daytime and went to college in the evenings. Today he is a chartered management accountant.

Two boys working within finance. That is amazing. Their mathematical ability does not come from me! I thank God he had a better plan for them than I had and for the way he enabled me to let them make their choices.

Easter Chicken and Scotty Bear may have retired but our home during those teenage years was neither quiet nor peaceful. "Burrr" was no longer heard but Roary the lion and Lippo the gorilla took over the fight and fight they could! I was told it was "friendly fighting" as they boisterously whacked each other over the head but at times it became apparent that all was not friendly. As they grew older their relationship deteriorated and I grieved as I remembered the prophecy for them at Kinmel Hall. Where was the close relationship foretold? If they were to be on different sides of the world but constantly spiritually close why were they fighting constantly in England? Was it all deception? Was it from God?

Charlie and Sam's problem was that they were so different. Blonde Charlie was quiet. Noisy Sam had dark hair. Charlie was very messy. Sam was immaculately tidy. Sam needed space, privacy, and independence. Charlie, who had at times had to act as a mother to Sam, could not let him go. Charlie is a people person and curious and his constant questioning of Sam's private life infuriated Sam. He had been so close to Sam and loved him, but he had to free him just as I had to.

The fighting became fiercer until one day it reached a head. It will never be forgotten and I am still amazed that something so small could cause such an outbreak.

Charlie knew just how, in a teasing way, he could annoy Sam and that day he excelled. I might have known that it was to be an unusual day. I had spent my inheritance on a small black car which Charlie, Sam, and I shared. There was often an argument over who should put in the petrol or who should move the car out of the way of John's car and Sam resented the fact that it was always him who cleaned the car. Charlie always left it to Sam. On this particular day, Charlie decided to clean the car to the amazement of all. When Charlie did a practical job he always did it well. The car was washed and waxed and gleaming. Sam began his tea as Charlie took the dustbuster off the wall and set about vacuuming the inside. As Sam was about to take his last mouthful, Charlie burst into the room with a naughty glint in his eye and I knew trouble was brewing.

"I've found a hairgrip in the car, Sam, and Mum does not wear hairgrips!" he announced, holding the offending object up for all to see.

It would be wrong of me to describe Sam's reaction in any detail, entertaining as it might be. Let us just say that furious was the understatement and leave it at that. Charlie fled to safety and I waited until Sam had calmed down.

"If I've got a girlfriend it's my own business." he complained to me.

I agreed and left the subject alone whilst suggesting to Charlie that he apologize, which he would not do.

A few days later when all was forgotten, I asked Sam about his friend.

"You can ask four questions," he graciously answered.

"Name?"

"Carol."

"Where did you meet?"

"Party."

"What does she look like?"

"Blonde."

"Would you bring her to see me?" hopefully.

"Might do".

End of conversation.

Chapter 22

Passing the Baton

I was more than surprised when two weeks later Sam told me that he would be taking Carol shopping and would bring her home for a cup of tea. It was a surprise because Sam does NOT do shopping, he hates it and also it was so soon after my allowance of four questions.

I remembered the first time I met John's mother. I was not nervous at all and put on no special act to impress. I just was myself and really hoped she would like me. Now in the mother's situation, I was so nervous. For a start I had no experience of girls. I grew up with a brother, my friends at school were the boys in the orchestra, I married John who had a younger brother, and all the Welton family seemed to produce boys. So, how do you "do" girls? I knew more about chinchillas than girls! I was out of my depth and it would have to be Sam to help me.

I sat in the comfy chair behind the door and waited to see what would walk through the door. I was safely hidden and my knees were actually knocking. I heard it before I saw it. The sound of the key in the door followed by a higher pitched voice asking, "Do we have to take our shoes off?"

"She must be blind," I thought. "Can't she see the age of our ancient carpet that told the tale of millions of filthy trainers and football boots that had worn it down over the years?"

After a little inaudible muttering, Sam walked through the door and announced, "This is Carol."

Carol entered the room, or rather half entered the room. Just a face peered round the door. Just as Sam had said, she was blonde. As her eyes met mine, the little soft voice inside me said,

"This is your daughter in law. Love her."

How ridiculous was my reaction, quickly followed by, "That's not God speaking, its just my thoughts. After all she is only seventeen and Sam is so young."

Carol took another step into the room and then I saw the expression on her face. I have never before or since seen anyone who looked so happy. She was happy, happy, happy! She was warm and friendly and we enjoyed a short time allowed by Sam and a cup of coffee. They left me bemused and feeling so privileged that Sam had allowed me into his private life, so much hidden from us.

"I shall wait and see," I decided.

Sam spent more and more time away from us with Carol, and Charlie saw less and less of him, growing more rejected and not understanding. At times emotions took over and self control faltered. Mistakes were made and our sons, foretold to be always there for one another, reached a rock bottom in their relationship. I grieved as I saw their love die and crumble and watched the misunderstandings and hurts turning into dislike then hatred. I was helpless. Suggestions of apologies were dismissed and suggestions of gestures towards healing were rejected.

I lost count of the hours, mounting into days and weeks that I cried out to Jesus for them and pleaded "Please Lord heal their broken relationship. I can't do it. It has to be you."

When Carol was eighteen, we were invited to her birthday barbecue. Charlie refused to have anything to do with it, fuelling even further the gulf between them. There we met her enormous family and learnt where her laugh came from. Her mother was an older "Happy Carol." Her father, cooking sausages, was drowning in sweat and charcoal but her beautiful eyes were unmistakably his.

Sam chose to go to university and was able to commute there, so often in the daytime he was at home working. Despite this, I felt I knew him less and less. He worked hour after hour in his little room and then in the evenings disappeared to his mystery world with Carol. At weekends he disappeared completely. It must have been hard for him to keep focussed because, try to hide it as I did, my health was going downhill worryingly. Inside the mystery Sam, the compassionate little boy who comforted me, was still there. He would leap down the stairs to carry in the shopping that was now too heavy for me, and as he flew past carrying packs of A4 paper I would feel a gentle quick rub on my back. Thank you, Sam. Jesus used you to get me through the hardest times.

As Sam disappeared, Charlie appeared, plodding stubbornly on and continuing to go to his church looking deeper and searching for the pieces of his life's jigsaw puzzle. He was hurting and the hurt served to push him towards Jesus even more. He could remember the miracle times but where were they now? He needed more.

I watched Carol support Sam through university and celebrate with us at his graduation. She was not happy when he was given a career opportunity to work away in London, but she knew it was an opportunity that only a fool would miss. She loved him enough to let him go even though it hurt her. It was not long though before the new salary paid for a sparkling ring on her finger and they were making wedding plans. They very much wanted to make all the arrangements themselves and even if they had wanted my help, I was too ill to help. I was spending my time in and out of hospitals having heart scans, angiograms, and endoscopies and praying

"Please Jesus let me live to see Sam marry. I don't mind missing the reception but please let me go to the church."

Sam chose to marry in the old Norman towered church where he said goodbye to his Grandpa and Grandma. They had married there and so had John and I, but I was most amazed that, without a word from me, Sam made this choice.

As Sam lived outside of the parish, he and Carol had to attend a weekly evening Anglican service for several months in order to legally marry there. Jesus said that where two or three people were together in his name he would be there with them and he was. Jesus knew Sam's needs and Sam said that in his hectic city life he found there a peace. He described it as "being soothed." That church and that peace have a special place in Sam and Carol's hearts.

Charlie was not involved in the wedding. There was no hired suit for him, no best man's place, no usher's duties. I had never liked my wedding dress and had always dreamt that if one of the boys married I would splash out and buy a really beautiful outfit for myself. It was a sight to be seen!

One week before the wedding day, a surprise guest arrived for the wedding. He was escorted to London by Charlie for a pre-arranged hotel meeting with a suspicious and puzzled Sam. It was Roary the lion. The reason it was such a surprise was that many years earlier, Sam, in a fury, threw him in the dustbin shouting "It's time we grew up, Charlie."

I had cried as the dustcart took him away the next day. No one knew that he had been rescued and washed by Charlie and hidden in an old unused picnic basket. Behind his closed bedroom door in secret Charlie had been making his own wedding preparations and here it was. Sam was presented with Roary, wearing a black dinner suit, white shirt, and black bow tie, all painstakingly hand stitched by Charlie. It was a small sign that the love was still there somewhere. It just needed Jesus to mend and he is in the healing and mending business!

Sam spent the night before his wedding day at home, his eyes sparkling with an excitement I had rarely seen. As bridegroom he was given the highest honour, "the priority of the bathroom!"

Dressed in his grey suit and pale blue cravat, he left for the church first. I knew I would be physically struggling and wanted plenty of time and so, supported by my elderly neighbour, Joan, we left after Sam to arrive next.

I stood looking up at the Norman bell tower and remembered our own wedding day, then Joan and I held hands and little at a time walked down the aisle. Ahead of me I could see the golden eagle Bible stand where a quivering eight-year-old Pam had been forced to read to the congregation. Looking up, I could see a golden hanging light with a red centre that my mother sometimes brought home to clean. There were so many memories.

"Do you mind if I sit on my own in a quiet pew?" asked Joan. She looked lovely and was dressed like the Queen Mother. She had lived next door to us since before the boys were born and I was so glad she was there. I settled her into a pew, wondering what pains were hidden behind her eyes.

I had no idea she was dying of cancer. She was so brave and hid her secret from all until a week before she died.

Without her physical support, I fixed my eyes on Sam at the front and hobbled down the aisle to my place at the front, clutching the handbag I had bought for Jim's wedding with one hand and holding on to my hysterectomy with the other. My shoes had been bought for a cousin's wedding twelve years earlier and because I had lost weight I had squeezed into a summer dress bought in the sale at the local cheap market. Yet, here was a miracle. I felt no resentment at the loss of my opportunity to wear a lovely outfit. All I felt was an overwhelming gratitude to be there and a happiness beyond the one that radiated from Carol's face,

In this enormous church, three of us were alone in silence with God, thinking our own thoughts. Sam turned round occasionally to see if anyone was arriving but most of the time he stood looking at the altar, his feet slightly apart and his hands clasped behind his back. I stared at him, the little squeally one now a man, knowing his own mind and being his own person. I thought of all that I had gone through to bring him up and of the painful cost of giving him the freedom God had required of me. I could see now how vital and important that had been, and would be in God's eternal plan.

I thought of my life. The Bible likens our lives to a race. What sort of race was mine? It was not a sprint. It felt like a marathon, gruelling, exhausting, pushing past barriers of pain, and yet it was not a marathon. A marathon has an exhilarating end with the crossing through the finishing line tape to loud cheers and applause. This was no marathon. Then I realized that my race was a relay race. It would continue as runners waiting took over from me. I had started the race carrying the baton of Jesus ready for the next generation. I had run with all the strength I had with John beside me.

Lost in my thoughts, I was only vaguely aware of guests arriving until the loud organ pipes burst forth in the familiar wedding march. I looked behind to see Carol looking so breath-taking, her rounded teenage cheeks transformed into the bone structure of a dignified beautiful young woman. I am sure I glimpsed a tear in her father's eyes. With all those we loved around us we listened as Sam and Carol made their vows. The vicar held their hands together in his and lifted them to God above them as he declared them to be man and wife. As he did so something happened in my heart. I passed the baton onto Sam saying in my heart

"Grab it, Sam and run with it. Run for all you are worth. Give the race all you have got. Ask and it will be given to you (even if you have to wait) seek and you will find. Jesus will never let you down and will keep his promises to you. Run, Sam, run!"

The baton is now in Sam's hand with his own race to run and with a generation only in the mind of God waiting to take it from him. Sam had left us and there was a feeling of completeness as he and Carol began their life together.

Chapter 23

⟋

On the Edge with God

Back at home, where once there had been four places at the table, now there were three, for John, myself, and a Charlie with an uncertain future. He needed to leave home but it was not the right time. Life became normal again. The phone would ring and I would go to answer it only to find it had disappeared, usually to be found under Charlie's duvet!

With Sam gone, Charlie filled his time with his large circle of friends, some old school friends like Dan, some work colleagues, and some church friends. In his usual way he plodded slowly on, thinking deeply, working hard in the daytime and evenings and searching. I knew studying was not easy for Charlie and I was so proud of him when we hung his chartered management accountant certificate on his wall. It was lovely to see how easily he made friends and how, in all work situations, he was loved and respected. He could relate to anyone, a gift from God that he would need. Despite his rewards for his diligence, there was an emptiness I could feel for him. There was a hunger for Jesus that was unsatisfied and I longed for him to have a special girl to share his life with.

All his life Charlie had dithered over decisions, to the frustration of all around. John's father can tell of the times he took Charlie and Sam to the sweet shop with their pocket money. Sam would glance his eye over the "pick and mix" and immediately choose his five sweets but fifteen minutes later, when everyone was inwardly screaming, Charlie had still not made up his mind. However, when eventually he did make a decision he usually sprung it on us as a sudden surprise. It was so one particular Sunday lunchtime as he drank his soup and ate his cheese.

"I've decided to get baptized next week on Easter Sunday," he announced as if he had chosen to wear a blue shirt. A decision so important and such a commitment for life and eternity mentioned so casually. All those years of questioning had now resulted in Charlie making his statement of faith in Jesus public. I knew that, as in all he did, that having committed to do something he would give it his all.

Jim and his family came to be with us as we listened to Charlie telling the story of his life's search, questions, and conclusion that all Jesus said is true. He had chosen Jesus. I heard of things I never knew and was surprised because I thought I knew Charlie inside out. One thing that was unusual about Charlie all his life was that from the age of one I could only remember him crying twice. Now I was sitting in the church on the front row listening and close enough to see a tear run down his face and rest collected in his spectacles as he said

"They broke my back."

How much more pain lay buried in Charlie, I wondered, and more worrying, how much had I caused?

Charlie meant his promise to follow Jesus wherever he was asked to go and soon he sprung another surprise.

"Mum, I have decided that I want to live on the edge with God," he told me with certainty and assurance. "I'm going to Australia."

Stunned was not an adequate word for how I felt.

"Are you sure?" I asked in my numbness.

"Yes."

"When?"

"I don't know. I'm praying about it. Pray for me," he asked.

I promised him my prayers and support but yet again there was the temptation to manipulate him to stay and the battle in my heart to let him go as I had let Sam go. Only if I did this would he achieve his potential. It was so hard.

It took a year for him to make his plans and he and I stood face to face as he lifted his suitcase and said, "Well, I suppose this is it."

We hugged and cried and I watched as his old car drove up the road we had walked so often together. Then he was gone.

I felt so alone and he looked so alone, going to the other side of the world and not knowing the future.

"Please, Jesus, don't let him be alone. If you will please give him a wife who will share his passion for you and who will understand his physical body and all he has gone through."

With that prayer I let him go and started to build my life without him.

Charlie phoned from time to time and as we talked it seemed impossible that he was at the other side of the world. He told me about his little flat and his church, about the delicious prawns and the barbecues. More than that, though he told me that, in Australia, he was experiencing the power of Jesus that he remembered as a child and so much wanted. He was excited and happy.

Charlie had one special friend, Ray. They had been close as teenagers ever since Charlie visited Ray in hospital after he had undergone an operation on his nose. Ray went to Sydney to visit Charlie and returned with interesting news. There was a special girl over there and Ray, probably without Charlie's permission, brought back the photographic evidence for me. In Ray's house I waited as his computer began to show me the sights of Australia and prepared to see the small, cuddly, motherly girl who seemed to be important to Charlie.

Do you know the saying, "You could have knocked me down with a feather?" This homely girlfriend was tall, slim, and stunningly beautiful, with long dark hair cascading down her back. The thought of Charlie with her was beyond my comprehension. She could have any man so why Charlie?

"Why Charlie?" I questioned Ray.

"Haven't a clue but she's good for him," he commented reassuringly.

It made no sense to me until the following Christmas when Charlie and Rachel returned to England for a few weeks for a visit to us and her family at the seaside. I had been instructed by those who knew better than I did, to prepare for "a top chick."

How do you get ready to face a posh, top chick?

I did my best. I bought a hand mirror for Sam's little bedroom so that she could attend to her stunning looks and I spent £3.99 on a tablecloth in a sale to cover the sun damaged varnish on our table.

Our first meeting was well planned in my mind but circumstances scattered my plans and I was thrown towards her in a flustered chaos.

Later, as I looked into her eyes, I saw that this stunning beauty was on the inside as well as the outside. Kindness, gentleness, thoughtfulness, and caring flowed out of her. I remembered my plea to Jesus as Charlie left. This young woman of such beauty was a Christian who shared Charlie's love of Jesus in his church. She was not only a Christian, she was a doctor! What an amazing answer to a mother's heart cry.

What a God!

How much God wanted to give Charlie that I would have robbed him of had I held onto him and not let him go. They were so happy together and Charlie was so changed. The miraculous things Jesus did in his life in that year, that are private to him, had given him a joy and freedom he never had before. He sparkled.

It was hard to say goodbye and see them return to Australia but within a few months, another of my sons had spent his pocket money on a sparkling ring. In Charlie's words, "Rachel is wearing a ring and a big smile."

I missed them, but I should have enjoyed the peace and rest because within a few months a wedding in England was being organized at high speed by emails and telephone calls. Three months before the wedding they returned and I found myself, as did Rachel's mother, covered in ivory card, burgundy ribbons, Bibles, and laptops.

So, where was Sam? He was commuting into the financial centre of London and recovering from shock. He and Carol came to meet Charlie and Rachel when they first came back at Christmas. Our room was not large and there were not enough comfy chairs for us all so Sam sat on the stool and Charlie sat at the other end of the room on a large comfy chair with Rachel on its arm drooped around Charlie's shoulders. The unfamiliar sight of Charlie in love was enough to shock us all but the shock for Sam came when Charlie leapt off his chair and hurtled himself towards Sam. Sensing emotion and urgency and expecting a fist to hit him, Sam shouted "No!" and defended his face with his arms. Ignoring his brother's cry of "No!" Charlie threw his arms round the confused Sam and sobbed his heart out. Never having faced such a situation before Sam instinctively, with the compassion he had possessed as a child, comforted Charlie who was dragged into the kitchen for some kitchen roll to dry his spectacles and for some tender loving medical care! To this day, I do not know what the tears were but I think they were a mixture of apology, hurt, and deep, deep love.

I had asked Jesus to mend their broken relationship and I cannot tell you how wonderful it was to see Carol and Rachel help them to repair the damage. Gradually in those who had been hurt forgiveness came and the process of daring to trust began. This is still a process ongoing today but now the words spoken over our sons at Kinmel Hall are true. They are often in other countries and far away, but they keep in touch and are ever growing closer. They will always be so different, but each strengthens the other and Rachel and Carol are beginning to build a friendship. Charlie now understands Sam's need to be with Carol as he needs to be with Rachel and the rejection has healed. It was my greatest sorrow to see them apart and my greatest joy to see their love being restored. It is the same love and support I saw in the hospital corridor as the two little figures in their furry duffel coats held hands as they needed each other. I am forever grateful to Carol and Rachel for their ongoing part in being used by Jesus to repair the damage and restore the love that Satan had wanted to destroy.

Ivory and burgundy, laptops and Bibles, snowdrops and roses. Wedding preparations were moving fast. "Was it because Australia is upside down that our house seemed upside down?" I wondered. In a small house it was difficult to find space. Two enormous cases containing all Charlie's worldly goods filled the front room and a neat compact bag belonging to Rachel lay in Sam's little room. I tried to give them as much space and privacy as I could, but they were happy to include us in all the joy they shared.

"Please can I come in?" I asked, considerately, knocking on Charlie's bedroom door.

"Sure," came the reply.

Confidently I walked in only to find an Australian usher face down on Charlie's bed, reading his Bible and drinking coffee. I never knew what to expect next! There were mugs everywhere, trainers under the coffee table, laughter and rage (as John once more lost the phone and had to search under the duvet!) Time flew. At Rachel's home by the sea, there was an even greater pile of preparations as Rachel's mother stumbled over happy, laughing small toddlers as she lovingly made icing flowers for the wedding cake she had made and ivory card became invitations and orders of service.

I had seen Charlie and Rachel sitting squeezed onto an armchair behind a laptop typing out their order of service, chosen with love and prayer over several weeks.

"Would you like to read it?" they asked, as their sparkling eyes indicated that they wanted me to see it. They passed me an ivory folded card with a burgundy rectangle surrounding a small silver heart in the centre. I had no idea of the content of Sam's service until it happened and it was exciting for me to have a preview.

Chapter 24

Order of Service

Welcome everyone (well, that had my OK).

Thank you all for coming and we hope that you will enjoy this time of celebrating with us and heaven as we tie the knot (This is a little different from Sam's).

Special thanks goes to our families and friends who have helped and supported us over the last few weeks and months and above all to Jesus for changing our lives and providing for us more than we ever imagined.

Love

Charlie and Rachel

It was clear from the introduction that this wedding was to be different and reflect Charlie and Rachel's own special story. I read on with interest until after "The Address" my stomach turned over.

"They can't have that hymn." I shouted inside myself inaudibly. They had chosen the hymn that I had always told John I wanted at my funeral. It was so special to me, summing up my life's purpose. Now they had got there first! I had no idea that they even knew it.

On a blustery November morning with a weather forecast of a rainy weekend, a car full of hired suits and a large hat box headed for the seaside. Yes, I did have my special outfit and to this day John has no exact idea of the cost. However, my dreams of posing like a star were again altered by God. He was not allowing pride a place. The photographer stood on the beach as gusty wind blew my elegant feminine skirt right through my knees, revealing for everyone for years and generations to come that my legs are not those of a model. My high heeled pewter shoes sank into the sand thrusting me backwards as the camera recorded it all. Charlie, as always calm and with a solution to a problem, found a way of putting his arm around me appearing as if he loved his mother greatly. Only he and I, and now you, know that he was holding on to my hat to prevent it being blown into the sea. My favourite photograph of the many taken that day is the one framed in our bedroom. It is of Charlie and Sam, side by side, wearing the same hire suits and sharing the most important day of Charlie's life. If a prophecy foretelling the future could have been photographed this was it. Through all the years, the duffel coats had been changed into wedding clothes.

The church nestling in amongst the evergreen forest was highlighted by cold November sunshine as baby buggies, pregnant sisters, toddlers clutching toys, and friends from all over the world gathered to await Rachel and her father. It seemed unreal and too good to be true

Charlie's wedding was unique and there was one special unusual moment. When the vicar asked, "Who gives this woman," it is usual for the bride's father to give her away. However, when the question was asked both Rachel's father and mother stepped forward and answered, "We do!" It was then that I gave Charlie away, passing the baton of our race into his willing and eager hand. As a relay racer does, I felt that at that moment I had pushed far beyond my ability right to the end and in my spirit I was falling forwards towards him to thrust the baton into his hand.

"Run with it Charlie. Go far, go near. Give it all you have got. Push beyond the limits you may feel you have. I am so proud of you and I respect and love you more than you'll ever understand."

I have run my race. I have reached my goal. The batons have been passed on and a new stretch of the race begins. My future, however long it may be, is safe in the hands of Jesus and I'll leave you to join us at Charlie's wedding and read the words of his wedding song, the story of my life and his future. If you can buy the music because it is so beautiful; then leave us and run your own unique race.

IN CHRIST ALONE by Keith Getty and Stuart Townend

In Christ alone my hope is found
He is my light, my strength, my song
This cornerstone, this solid ground
Firm through the fiercest drought and storm
What heights of love, what depths of peace
When fears are stilled, when strivings cease
My Comforter, my All in All
Here in the love of Christ I stand.

In Christ alone, who took on flesh
Fullness of God in helpless babe
This gift of love and righteousness
Scorned by the ones He came to save
Til on that cross as Jesus died
The wrath of God was satisfied
For every sin on Him was laid
Here in the death of Christ I live.

There in the ground His body lay
Light of the world by darkness slain
Then bursting forth in glorious Day
Up from the grave He rose again
And as He stands in victory
SIN'S CURSE HAS LOST ITS GRIP ON ME
For I am his and He is mine
Bought with the precious blood of Christ.

No guilt in life, no fear in death
This is the power of Christ in me
From life's first cry to final breath
Jesus commands my destiny
No power of hell, no scheme of man
Can ever pluck me from His hand
Till He returns or calls me home
Here in the power of Christ I'll stand.

For communications concerning this book
or to order copies please contact:
marmsspg@aol.com